The Adirondacks
Forever Wild   by George Wuerthner

© 1988 American Geographic Publishing
Helena, Montana
William A. Cordingley, Chairman
Rick Graetz, Publisher
Mark Thompson, Director of Publications
Barbara Fifer, Assistant Book Editor

NEW YORK
GEOGRAPHIC SERIES

Number 1

Front cover photo: *View into the High Peaks area.* TOM TILL
Title page: *Dawn over South Meadow near Adirondak Loj.*
GEORGE WUERTHNER
Left: *Marcy Dam, High Peaks Wilderness.* GEORGE WUERTHNER
Bottom left: *Roaring Brook Falls near St. Huberts.* GEORGE WUERTHNER
Bottom right: *Atop Whiteface Mountain.* CLYDE H. SMITH
Facing page: *Ausable Lakes from Indian Head Lookout.* GERARD LEMMO
Page 5: *Lake Placid.* GEORGE WUERTHNER
Back cover, left: *Potsdam sandstone along the Ausable River.* TOM TILL
Right: *Lake Clear near Paul Smith's.* GEORGE WUERTHNER

Library of Congress Cataloging in Publication Data

Wuerthner, George.
The Adirondacks: forever wild.

(New York geographic series ; no. 1)
1. Adirondack Park (N.Y.)   2. Adirondack Mountains (N.Y.)--
Description and travel.   I. Title.   II. Series.
F127.A2W84   1988   974.7'5304   88-6157
ISBN 0-938314-44-0 (pbk.)

ISBN 0-938314-44-0
© 1988 American Geographic
Publishing
Box 5630, Helena, MT 59604
(406) 443-2842

Text © 1988 George
Wuerthner.

Cover by Len Visual Design.

Book design by Linda McCray.

Printed in Hong Kong.

ACKNOWLEDGMENTS AND DEDICATION

A great many individuals contributed indirectly or directly to this book, including other book and magazine authors whose works I used as reference material. It would be impossible to acknowledge all their work here, but to them, I owe a debt of gratitude. For those interested in a more detailed view of the Adirondacks, I would suggest these titles: *The Adirondack Park: A Political History*, by Frank Graham, Jr.; *Adirondack Wilderness: A Story of Man and Nature*, by Jane Eblen Keller; *Land Acquisition for New York State: A Historical Perspective*, by Norman J. Van Valkenburgh; and *Adirondack Country*, by William Chapman White. In addition, I would like to thank Bradford B. VanDiver for his assistance with geology, George Davis for his visionary view of the Adirondacks, and the staff of the Adirondack Park Agency in Ray Brook, who provided with much useful information concerning the park's history and land use regulations. In addition, there were many other individuals—fishermen, librarians, backpackers, and Chamber of Commerce representatives—who each in his own way contributed to my knowledge of the Adirondack region, and to them I owe a huge thank-you.

I dedicate this book to my parents, George and Mildred Wuerthner, who encouraged my early interest in nature and allowed me to freely pursue my love of the outdoors, which has taken me throughout North America and brought me full circle back again to the Adirondack Mountains.

ABOUT THE AUTHOR

Writer-photographer-naturalist George Wuerthner has been employed as a university instructor in California, a surveyor in Wyoming, a wilderness ranger in Alaska, and a botanist in Idaho. He has backpacked, skied, kayaked and canoed extensively in wild places from Mexico to Alaska. His writing and photography have appeared in many natural-history and outdoor publications and he has written three other books in the American Geographic Series.

LAND USE CLASSIFICATIONS

Land classifications under the Adirondack Park State Land Master Plan adopted in 1979. There are nine *public-land* categories in all. The vast majority of the state lands are designated as either wilderness or wild forest.

Wilderness—areas more than 10,000 acres in size without noticeable human intrusions. No motorized vehicles allowed.

Primitive—areas less than 10,000 acres, but in other ways similar to wilderness except that certain human intrusions presently exist, eventually to be removed.

Canoe—Only one at present—St. Regis Canoe area—managed same as wilderness.

Wild Forest—Similar to wilderness, but motorized access permitted along with other human intrusions like fire towers, ranger stations, etc.

Intensive Use—Campgrounds, boat-launch sites, ski areas.

Historic Areas—Two areas: Crown Point and John Brown's Farm.

Travel Corridors—Roadbed and land visible from roadways.

Administrative—includes prisons, police stations, Adirondack Park Agency offices, etc.

Classification of *private lands* in the Adirondack Park Land Use and Development Plan adopted in 1973.

Hamlet—present townsites within park. No limit placed on lot size or number of buildings. Future development is encouraged here.

Moderate Intensity Use—Suitable for intense development, primarily residential. A 1.3-acre lot size required and no more than 500 buildings per square mile are allowed.

Low Intensity Use—Land suitable for a lower degree of development. Average lot size must be 3.5 acres and no more than 200 buildings per square mile are permitted.

Rural Use—Low level of development—protection of open space important. Lot size must be 8.5 acres and no more than 75 buildings are permitted per square mile.

Resources Management—Mostly agriculture or forest lands. Lot size must be 42.7 acres. No more than 15 buildings per square mile.

Industrial—Mining or factories. No limits imposed.

Legend:
- Wilderness
- Wild Forest
- Canoe Area

CONTENTS

INTRODUCTION

Above: *Cattails along Brant Lake.*
Right: *The 6-million-acre Adirondack State Park is the largest state park in the country, and bigger than most national parks. Within these boundaries, one could fit nearly three Yellowstone National Parks. Seen here is Blue Mountain Lake.*
GEORGE WUERTHNER PHOTOS

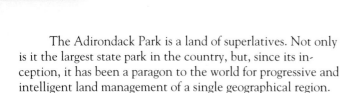

The Adirondack Park is a land of superlatives. Not only is it the largest state park in the country, but, since its inception, it has been a paragon to the world for progressive and intelligent land management of a single geographical region.

It was not always this way. The Adirondack region once suffered: its wildlife populations were ravaged and the magnificent forests were turned into lumber and pulp. But, unlike the trend in most parts of the globe, this destruction has been reversed and the Adirondacks have been slowly healing. If anything, they are wilder now than they were just 50 years ago and, though surrounded by millions of people, the region has become a paradigm of how people can enjoy a landscape, and protect and preserve the biological foundations that make it special.

CREATION OF THE PARK

The original Adirondack Park was created in 1892 when the New York State Legislature created a 2.8-million-acre preserve in the heart of the Adirondack Mountains. A legislatively mandated study commission delineated this area on a map by a blue line. The "Blue Line" became the accepted term for the park boundaries. Since its original inception, the size of the park has been increased several times so that by 1983 the area within the Blue Line encompassed nearly 6 million acres. This represents approximately one fifth of New York State's 30.2 million acres and is roughly equal in size to the state of Vermont. It is by far the largest state park in the country and larger than most national parks. Yellowstone National Park, for example, contains 2.2 million acres.

WATER, WATER EVERYWHERE

Although recreation always has been a major Adirondack activity, the original park was established for watershed protection. The headwaters for five major basins—the Mohawk, Hudson, St. Lawrence, Black and Lake Champlain—are found here. Water characterizes this region and it seems to weep and ooze from the ground everywhere. Nearly 15 percent of the park is considered wetland of some kind and within the park's borders are some 2,800 ponds and lakes, and more than 30,000 miles of brooks, streams and rivers. Lake Champlain, sixth largest freshwater lake in the country, forms part of the eastern border of the park, although only a portion of the lake is actually within the park borders. Plenty of lakes are totally within the park boundaries, including 32-mile-long Lake George, and Long and Indian lakes.

Part of the reason for the range's ability to wring water from clouds has to do with its overall height. The Adirondacks contain more than 100 peaks above 3,500′ in elevation, and more than 40 peaks that rise above 4,000′. Mt. Marcy, at 5344′, is the state's highest summit and one of the highest peaks on the East Coast.

The Adirondacks gain more than a mile in elevation between Lake Champlain at 95′ above sea level and Mt. Marcy's summit, and the average elevation of this uplift is 1500′, thus presenting a formidable mountain barrier to the passage of weather systems. In the Northeast, only the White Mountains in New Hampshire have a comparable extent of highlands. So the Adirondacks are rainier, and snowier, than most of the state—and colder: in 1934 the New York State record low of minus 52° was recorded at Stillwater along the western edge of the park.

ECONOMIC TRENDS

The severe climate, coupled with poor soils, limited transportation and seasonal economic opportunities have restricted population growth. Today the area supports about 120,000 people, compared to 104,000 more than a hundred

The region has become a paradigm of how people can enjoy a landscape, and protect and preserve the biological foundations that make it special.

Ausable River near Keene. CLYDE SMITH

7

years ago. This is the biggest region in New York State without a single city—its largest population centers are Saranac Lake, Tupper Lake and Lake Placid. Hamilton County, which includes Long and Indian lakes, has only a few more than 5,000 people and a population density of just 2.9 people per square mile. The population density for the area within the Blue Line is 11.3 people per square mile, which compares with some wide-open areas of the West.

On the fringes of the park, farming has been a marginal proposition, but during the 1800s, it was one of the leading occupations. In 1910 Warren County had 1,865 farms, which covered 44.5 percent of its area, but by 1969, the area devoted to agriculture had been reduced to 0.6 percent. Except for the Lake Champlain lowlands, most of the farm acreage in the rest of the region also has decreased that dramatically.

Logging was another major occupation during the early years of Adirondack history. In 1872, before the peak in logging activity, some 1,069,000 market logs were floated down the Hudson to mills. But this was cut-and-run forestry, and the industry folded as the easily accessible timber petered out. Timber harvest continues today, however, and some areas are actually being cut for the second or third time. Tree growth in this austere environment is slow compared to other regions of the country, and it is doubtful that the harvest levels of the 1800s ever will be repeated. At present some 70 percent of the park is forested with some 30 species of trees. Because of the Forever Wild clause of the state constitution, which forbids cutting trees on state Forest Preserve lands, the percentage of tree cover likely will continue to increase.

Mining flourished in the early years of the European occupation and a few towns like Port Henry, Tahawus and North Creek owe their existence to the mining of iron, garnets and other ores. But as better ore deposits were discovered farther west, mining, like farming, declined and only the garnet mine near Gore Mountain continues to operate.

OWNERSHIP PATTERNS

The park encompasses parts or all of twelve counties including Oneida, Hamilton, Essex, Franklin, St. Lawrence, Herkimer, Warren, Lewis, Fulton, Saratoga, Clinton and Washington. Following the New England tradition, these counties are further divided into townships or "towns"

Left: More than half the Adirondack Park is privately owned, a large percentage by timber companies, and timber harvest continues today. GEORGE WUERTHNER
Below: At one time farming dominated the economies of communities on the fringes of the Adirondacks. For example, in 1910 Warren County had 1,865 farms that covered 44.5 percent of its area. By 1969 this had shrunk to 0.6 percent. ALBERT GATES *Facing page: The Adirondacks have 30,000 miles of streams and rivers, 2,800 lakes. This is Marcy Brook.* GEORGE WUERTHNER

By the turn of the century, the number-one Adirondack industry was tourism.

containing communities usually referred to as villages. Sometimes a single village sits astride one or more towns. For example, the village of Saranac Lake is partially within three towns: North Elba, Harrietstown, and St. Armand.

The Blue Line marks the boundaries of the park found in these counties, but not all the land within its boundaries is owned by the state. In fact, only 40 percent is presently part of the state holdings, called the Forest Preserve; the remainder is held by private owners including timber companies, clubs and individuals. As originally conceived, all the private lands within the park borders were to be acquired as park land, but that goal was soon abandoned as impractical. Thus the park is really a patchwork of public and private lands.

Residents within the Blue Line and those living elsewhere in the state are embroiled in a seemingly endless debate over development appropriate for both state-owned and privately-held lands. Because of the overlapping political jurisdictions and ownership patterns, cohesive and uniform codes governing the management of both public and private holdings were nearly impossible. By the late 1960s, some people felt that the beauty and biological integrity of the Adirondacks were threatened unless one governmental unit supervised all the area within the Blue Line. Thus, in 1972 the Adirondack Park Agency.

Area residents generally were not supportive of the new agency. As with so many conservation measures, the primary support for the creation and continued existence of the park has come from outside, in this case particularly from New York's city dwellers. Even at its inception, support for the park idea came from businessmen who saw the Adirondacks as a source of water for commerce (including the operation of canals), and from city residents who sought a mountain refuge from the pressures of urban living.

RECREATION INDUSTRY

Today, though watershed protection still is a primary reason for the the park, recreation constitutes the major use of the region. Nearly from its initial discovery by Europeans, the Adirondacks have been considered an outdoor recreation paradise. Early visitors returned with tales of good deer hunting, catches of big trout, canoe trips on beautiful rivers, and stories about the invigorating life available to any citybound person who could afford a vacation in the mountains. By the turn of the century the number-one Adirondack industry was tourism. Today a visitor to the Adirondacks has a spectrum of outdoor activities available. He or she can raft whitewater in the Hudson River Gorge, ski the runs at Whiteface Mountain, snowmobile at Old Forge, canoe the St. Regis Lakes, climb the High Peaks, hunt, fish, hike, sail, swim, picnic, or simply sit on the porch of a cabin or hotel and just watch the water. For those who don't relish the outdoor life, there are miles of scenic highways worthy of exploration by car.

The state maintains dozens of public boat launching ramps, campgrounds and hiking, ski, snowmobile, canoe and horse trails. One can climb to the top of Mt. Marcy or drive to the top of Whiteface. In the evening, it's dining on trout caught fresh from a back-country pond, or on lobster from a Lake George restaurant. Overnight accommodations vary from island campsites in Lake George to bed-and-breakfasts in Keene Valley.

In addition to state-financed facilities, there are many privately operated ones, such as the Adirondack Museum at Blue Mountain Lake, Fort Ticonderoga and the Forest Industries Exhibit Hall in Old Forge. Within or near the park's borders are 36 additional museums.

Above: Hikers on Whiteface, High Peaks Wilderness. JERI WRIGHT
Right: Since most of the acreage within Adirondack Park once was logged, the park is in effect an experiment in ecosystem restoration, where natural processes are allowed to continue without undue manipulation by humans, as here in the East Branch of the Ausable River. GEORGE WUERTHNER

The people of New York have said they want to determine the future of the Adirondacks intelligently.

But the value of the Adirondacks goes well beyond recreational use. No larger piece of real estate on the East Coast has been devoted primarily to preservation of scenic and ecological values. The laws establishing the Adirondack Forest Preserve, as part of the state constitution, represent the strongest protection against unwise development ever bestowed upon any land area in the country. Even our national park system has less stringent regulations. In addition, the area within Blue Line represents, as completely as any political boundary ever can, an entire bioregion. Again, there is no precedent for this anywhere in the nation. Even our best examples of national parks lack some essential biological components within their politically drawn borders, and thus do not represent a complete ecosystem under one land management agency.

But merely having a boundary around a bioregion does not guarantee it will survive intact as an ecological unit. Two master land use plans had to be developed., one for some 40 percent of the park that is public land and the other for private lands. These represent the first successful attempt anywhere to integrate land use planning over an entire biological-physiological region. In essence, the people of New York have said that they want to determine the future of the Adirondacks intelligently.

The constitutional protection afforded the Adirondacks guarantees that in the future they not only will look as they do today, but may in fact be wilder. The people of New York State have given themselves a beautiful and enjoyable park, and they have bequeathed to future generations a gift that will grow in value and importance—a wild and biologically intact ecosystem that will continue to provide for physical as well as spiritual needs.

WEATHER

The Adirondacks, as a highlands, catch more than their share of weather. Situated as the first mountains encountered by weather patterns coming from the west, the Adirondacks are cloudy, and wetter than surrounding lowlands. In addition, precipitation in the lee of these mountains along Lake Champlain is less than on the western slope.

But the major climatic factor influencing the Adirondacks is cold. Below-freezing temperatures are recorded for about 190 days or more a year, and temperatures of zero or below on an average of 39 days, at such representative Adirondack communities as Lake Placid and Tupper Lake. Surprising to some people is that the coldest winter temperatures occur in the high mountain basins, rather than on the peaks. This is borne out by weather records taken at Lake Placid and Whiteface Mountain. The average daily minimum temperature for Lake Placid is 28.9° while the weather station at 4,866' on top of Whiteface Mountain is a startlingly five degrees warmer at 34.0°. Towns like Tupper Lake and Lake Placid have recorded lows of minus 38° and minus 37° respectively and the coldest recording for the Adirondacks as well as the state is held by the small town of Stillwater on the western edge of the park where in 1934 a temperature of minus 52° was observed (endured).

Because of the often below-freezing temperatures, snow cover is a common feature of the landscape, lasting an average of 105 days a year in the central Adirondacks. More than 100" of the white stuff falls in the normal year and a record of 167" was recorded for Lake Placid in the big snow winter of 1970-1971.

Annual precipitation for the central Adirondacks is in the neighborhood of 38" to 39", higher in the southwest part of the park and lower beyond the High Peaks region. Winter is definitely the cloudiest time of the year with only about 40 percent sunshine.

But summer is when most people visit the Adirondacks, and then the average coolness is a pleasure. While many lowland areas swelter in high humidity and temperatures, in the Adirondacks the highest temperatures do not even reach 90°. Night-time temperatures average in the 50s or even lower, making it extremely pleasant for sleeping. On the average summer afternoon, the temperature will be a pleasant 70° to 80°.

Snow is a fact of life in the Adirondacks. In the central Adirondacks, the ground remains snow-covered an average of 105 days of the year. The cool average temperature made the uplands unsuitable for most agricultural enterprises, but perfect as a summertime escape from lowland heat. This is one reason the region always has been attractive as a summer recreation area. GEORGE WUERTHNER

GEOLOGY

1

A satellite view of the Adirondacks shows the roughly circular pattern of these mountains, with the highest point in the right central region we call the High Peaks. Surrounding the High Peaks is hilly country that gradually falls off to lowlands on all sides

FAULTS & DRAINAGES

Also readily observable is the crisscrossed drainage scheme dominated by several bold northeast-southwest–trending valleys and ranges. This pattern marks the location of faults or breaks in the earth's crust where giant masses of rock have been displaced. Such movement is usually imperceptible, but sometimes shows itself suddenly and violently in an earthquake. Although most of the present fault pattern was established millions of years ago, movement along these crustal breaks still is occurring: the ground-shaking near Blue Mountain Lake in 1983, for example, measured 5.2 on the Richter Scale.

Since water always seeks the lowest and easiest route through any rock mass, rivers and streams tend to follow these fault patterns inscribed on the earth's crust. For example, the Indian River flows northward to meet the south-flowing Hudson at Cedar Ledges, both following the same northeast-trending fault. After the Indian River joins the Hudson, the Hudson makes a 90° turn to the east again, following another fault. Some of these linear fault valleys are filled by long, narrow lakes or strings of lakes—like Indian, Long and Ausable.

A view from space also would show long trough-like depressions resulting when a block of the crust drops relative to the rock faces on either side of it, forming what is called a *graben* (from the German for grave). Lake George occupies a graben.

These patterns, like the scars on the face of a boxer, tell us something about the Adirondacks' geological history, and record the past battles between geological forces. They also allow us to make certain predictions about the region's future.

IN THE BASEMENT

A wide variety of rocks makes up the Adirondacks region, but the core of the range, visible in the High Peaks and elsewhere, are ancient *metamorphic* (metamorphic means to change) rocks. Some 1.1 billion years old, they form the Precambrian (before life) basement rocks, core of the North America continent. In most places the basement rocks are covered by younger sedimentary and *igneous* rocks ("of fire," such as rocks erupted from volcanoes). Only in a few places in the world are basement rocks exposed at the surface. One of such expanse includes much of eastern Canada, with one sub-unit that reaches into northeast New York as the Adirondacks. This massive rock outcrop is known as the Canadian Shield. The youngest, easternmost portion of the Shield is called the Grenville Province, the southeast toe of which extends into New York State, cropping out in the Thousand Islands region as well as in the Adirondack Mountains.

Despite the age of these Precambrian basement rocks, their exposure in the Adirondack Mountains is a relatively recent phenomenon. Erosion leveled the Adirondacks long ago, but recent mountain-building activity has uplifted the roots of this ancient range and exposed them anew.

This uplift continues today at a rate of three millimeters per year. Surprisingly, this rate, is rather rapid compared to uplift rates elsewhere. Over the last million years this region has risen three kilometers or about 10,000'. Erosion, meanwhile, continues to wear down the Adirondacks, but the very hard basement rocks that comprise the range's core are exceedingly resistant to erosive forces, and remain as the prominent peaks we see today.

Fault patterns, like the scars on the face of a boxer, tell us something about the Adirondacks' geological history, and record the past battles between geological forces.

*Hull Brook Flume near Keene.
Flumes are created when the basement
rock is intruded by a softer rock.
Because it is softer than adjacent
material, it is more rapidly eroded by
water and hence creates narrow gorges
as seen here.* GEORGE WUERTHNER

continental masses change position and shape—for example, North America was once attached to Europe and the Atlantic Ocean did not exist at all. The energy that fuels plate movements comes from radioactive decay deep in the earth, which sets up convection currents that slowly circulate molten rock just beneath the crust, rafting pieces of continental plate with it.

Long ago, hundreds of millions of years before present, when there was no life on land, and barely any except algae in the sea, the area now comprising the Grenville Province lay under a sea. Sand, mud and clay eroded from an adjacent continent was deposited into the still ocean waters. These layers of sediments gradually hardened into what geologists call sedimentary rocks, eventually thousands of feet thick.

While these sediments were accumulating, two continental masses were drifting toward each other. As they moved closer, the denser rock of the intervening ocean basin gradually slid under the lighter continental rocks so that, by 1300 million years ago, the ocean basin had completely disappeared and the two continental plates crashed together. The force of this collision crumpled adjacent rocks into a lofty mountain range sometimes called the Grenville Mountains, which can be thought of as the ancestral Adirondacks.

These ancient mountains stretched along the entire coast of this early continent. Intense pressure and heat accompanied the plate suture, and sedimentary rocks along the margins were squeezed, melted and changed, or metamorphosed as geologists say, into new kinds of rock—often harder and more uniform in composition than the original sedimentary materials. For approximately 650 million years, these two continents remained welded together. All the while, erosion was stripping away surface materials and reducing the once-great mountain range to a lowland, the hard, crystalline roots of the Grenville Mountains.

ANCIENT SEABEDS

Approximately 650 million years ago, a new ocean basin began to develop east of the Grenville Province and a shallow arm of the ocean, the Potsdam Sea, gradually covered much of what is now New York State. Sediments accumulated along the shore, burying the old roots of the Grenville Mountains. Remnants of these sediments today are exposed in a number places. One of the easiest places to see them is in the Ausable River Chasm, where the Ausable has cut into the ancient seabeds of the Potsdam Sea. If you hike down into the gorge,

PLATE TECTONICS

Geologists believe that the surface of the earth is composed of individual plates that are constantly moving apart or smashing into each other as they float about earth's mantle like chunks of ice in a partially frozen river. This is called the theory of plate tectonics. Over time, pieces of these

it's easy to distinguish the different sedimentary layers since they appear stacked—like pages of a book. Some of these exposed "pages" even sport fossil ripple marks, frozen in rock for millions of years but looking so fresh that one might suppose they were created just days ago.

Sandstones like those at Ausable Chasm usually were deposited close to shore in shallow water, one reason for the ripple marks. As the Potsdam Sea gradually spread over more of the land, different sedimentary deposit—such as limestones and dolostone known as the Theresa Formation—were laid down in deeper waters farther from shore. Other marine sedimentary rocks, even younger, include the Ogdensburg Dolomite and Chazy limestones, which includes fossil reef formations—each formation named for the location where it was first described.

The occurrence of fossil coral reefs indicates a warm tropical environment, and plate tectonics provides an explanation for this oddity. One must remember that the pieces of the earth's crust that make up the continental masses are continuously moving about the globe and that their present positions are no indication of past ones. During the time when the Chazy Limestones were deposited, the continental plate was much farther south, closer to the equator.

MOUNTAIN-BUILDING

The deposition of sediments into this marine environment continued for millions of years. Then, sometime around 445 million years ago, there was a reversal in the convection currents that controlled the movement of continental plates. The plates began to converge and the ocean basin gradually disappeared under the edge of a crustal plate. A new mountain system began to form along the eastern edge of today's New York. One eroded remnant of this mountain-building period we know today as the Taconic Range. During this geological episode, the mountain-building east of the Adirondack region stretched the earth's crust and created many block faults in the Adirondacks, particularly along their eastern margin. These are visible today as the cross-hatching so prominent on satellite images. Bedrock was crushed along these fault zones, hastening erosion. As a result, many of the narrow valleys that separate higher peaks—such as the Avalanche Pass and Indian Pass region of the High Peaks—mark these crustal breaks.

In addition, these cracks or zones of crustal weakness frequently were filled by intrusions of molten rock that subsequently hardened to form what geologists call *dikes*. In the High Peaks region where the country rock is very hard, the softer intruded rock was eroded faster—creating very narrow, slot-like drainages locally called *flumes*. Hull Brook Flume near Keene owes its origins to one of these intruded dikes.

EROSION

The Adirondack region nearly was leveled by erosion during the millions of years since the beginning of the Taconic mountain-building period. The Taconic *orogeny* (a

Sedimentary rocks surround the fringes of the Adirondack uplift and once covered even the hard basement rocks that now are exposed in the High Peaks and elsewhere. Seen here are fossilized ripples in the Potsdam Sandstone, a sedimentary rock exposed by erosion of the Ausable River at Rainbow Falls. GEORGE WUERTHNER

Some of these exposed "pages" even sport fossil ripple marks, frozen in rock for millions of years but looking so fresh that one might suppose they were created just days ago.

geological term for mountain uplift) was followed by additional mountain-building episodes to the east and south—the Acadian and Alleghenian orogenies—resulting from the final convergence of the North American continental plate with Europe and Africa. During the Acadian orogeny, the granites that eventually would make up the White Mountains of New Hampshire were intruded and, during the Alleghenian period, the folding of rock strata that created the Appalachian Mountains took place, but these events had no major impact upon the Adirondack region, according to present interpretation.

A relatively quiet period in Adirondack geological history ensued for several hundred million years, during which the North American plate once again reversed direction and began to separate from Europe and Africa, with the present Atlantic Ocean opening behind it.

UPLIFT

Beginning about 25 million years ago (a very rough guess) the Adirondack region once more was uplifted into its present dome shape. Geologists believe a hot spot, or *plume*, of molten rock lying close to the earth's surface under the Adirondack region is responsible for this uplift.

The greatest uplift is near the center of the dome, in the region we call the High Peaks. The greatest erosion stripping of rock material has occurred in this central area, and nearly all the original sedimentary deposits that once covered the ancient mountain roots have been removed.

The High Peaks' exposed basement rocks are composed of anorthosite, a metamorphic rock of nearly homogeneous and uniform strength. Anorthosite is formed by the metamorphosis of sedimentary rocks deep in the Earth—as much as 15 miles down—which gives an idea of how much uplift and erosion had to occur before these rocks were exposed.

One can think of the Adirondack dome as layers in an onion sliced across the upper third to expose part of its core—the anorthosite and the original country rock into which it was intruded—surrounded by progressively younger rocks such as the Potsdam sandstones that form the outer skin. Erosion continues to peel away the younger rocks, exposing more of the basement anorthosite.

ICE AGE

The last major event in the Adirondacks' geological history began less than 2 million years ago when vast ice sheets formed over the earth's poles, beginning the Ice Age.

Eventually the accumulations of snow became so great that ribbons of ice began to squeeze outward like toothpaste from a tube. Massive ice sheets flowed southward and then retreated northward on at least four occasions, the last one ending only 6,000 years ago. At one time glacial ice covered nearly all of what is Canada and much of the northern United States, including the Adirondack region.

The last major glacial advance, called the Wisconsin glaciation, reached its peak approximately 18,000 to 20,000 years ago and ice was perhaps 6,000 feet thick in the Adirondack region—deep enough to bury even the highest peaks under an icy cloak.

Acting like a giant bulldozer, these southward-flowing glaciers straightened valleys, gouged basins, and scraped away much of the topsoil that once covered the Adirondack peaks. They also plucked rocks and boulders from the bedrock, some of which became embedded in the glacier. This debris transformed the ice flows into giant rasps, which smoothed off rocky knobs and protuberances—leaving the north slopes rounded like whale's backs, while ripping rocks from the south faces and creating cliffs.

As the ice forced its way through the valleys between peaks, it ground off protruding knobs, steepened the sides and flattened the bottoms. These glaciated valleys exhibit a U-shaped appearance in cross-section, the classic sign of the glacier action. Examples of such valleys abound in the Adirondacks, including Indian Pass Brook and the Ausable Lakes Valley.

The unsorted rocky material which a glacier picks up and carries, or bulldozes to its sides and snout, is called *moraine*. This morainal load often appears today as low hills that contain unsorted gravels, boulders and rocks all mixed together. The village of Lake Placid is built upon one of these glacial moraines, which also dams the waters of Lake Placid itself.

But low morainal hills are not the only legacy of the Ice Age found in the Adirondacks. Perhaps the most important result of the glaciers was the creation of the thousands of lakes and ponds that now dot the Adirondack landscape. These lakes were created by morainal damming—as with Lake Placid, Lake George and Indian Lake—or by a basin gouged from bedrock subsequently filling with water—as is the case with some of the Fulton Chain Lakes.

Glaciers even changed drainage patterns. When you drive southwest from the village of Blue Mountain Lake you pass over a barely perceptible mound that separates two major

Top: Lake George occupies a fault-bounded basin called a graben, which was deepened by glacial action. As the continental ice sheet retreated, it left a moraine that dammed the lake. The village of Lake George, seen here, is built upon this glacial moraine.
Left: The hollow bowl-shaped basins on Dix Mountain, the prominent peak on the horizon, are cirques carved by glacial action. In the foreground, bedrock smoothed by the rasping of continental glaciers.
Facing page: Geologists speculate that about 25 million years ago the Adirondack dome began its most recent uplift. This has rejuvenated rivers, increasing their rate of descent, so that rapids and waterfalls are common in the park. Sedimentary rock layers like pages in a book are evident in this photo of the Ausable River Chasm. GEORGE WUERTHNER PHOTOS

19

watersheds—the Hudson and St. Lawrence. Blue Mountain Lake now drains to the St. Lawrence River via the Raquette River system, but once it flowed east into Lake Durant and eventually the Hudson River. This old pathway has been blocked by a low hill of glacial debris, so today the lake waters take a much more circuitous route to the Atlantic via the St. Lawrence—all because of a small pile of moraine the casual observer hardly notices.

Eskers are another relatively rare, but notable, glacial feature of the Adirondacks. These low, snake-like ridges of sand and gravel mark the courses of streambeds that once flowed on top of, or inside, large glacial ice sheets. Although not common, they are most noticeable in the northwest portion of the Adirondacks, where relief is low and fragments of the huge ice sheets lay stagnant for a long time before melting away. Well known eskers are found along Lower Saranac Lake, in the Five Ponds Wilderness and at Star Lake west of Cranberry Lake. Since the gravels and sand that make up eskers usually are well drained, they often are covered with drought-resistant plant species like eastern white pine.

Moraines and eskers often are difficult for the untrained eye to discern, but one glacial feature seen frequently by those who climb the region's peaks is the *erratic*. As their name implies, erratics are rock fragments that appear out of place. These fragments, usually boulders, are picked up by glacial ice and transported to a new location where they are dropped during glacial retreat. Frequently these boulders rest on peaks and slopes and obviously are not weathered out of the surrounding bedrock. Erratics are common on all the higher peaks including Mt. Marcy, and provide one sure piece of evidence that these peaks once were covered by glaciers.

Because of the tremendous amount of meltwater resulting during the retreat of the ice sheets, many temporary lakes were formed wherever drainage was blocked by moraine or ice. Old wave-cut shorelines and smooth sediment plains resulting from these temporary lakes are visible throughout the region. The nearly level expanse of the Keene Valley was once the bottom of one of these glacial lakes. Another notable example is the wide-open expanse of fields along the road leading to Adirondak Loj just south of Lake Placid. The rich soils deposited as sediments on the lake bottom created this fertile plain. Along the road leading to the lodge, a number of erratics seen along the edge of the fields, likely were rafted here on icebergs that subsequently grounded and melted, leaving their rocky burdens.

Most of these glacial lakes were short-lived, and some were quite large. For example, along the New York-Vermont border in the trough-like Champlain Basin, a huge glacial lake once existed, many times greater than today's Lake Champlain. Its ancient wave-cut benches still are evident on the surrounding mountains. Because the retreating ice sheet blocked drainage to the north via the St. Lawrence River, water from the melting ice flooded most of the Champlain lowlands and cut an outlet south to the Hudson River.

Eventually the ice sheets occupying the Champlain Basin retreated farther north, but instead of the lake water's draining out to the St. Lawrence, salt water poured in and created the Champlain Sea. Due to the tremendous weight of the glacial ice sheets, the earth beneath them had been depressed hundreds of feet. Once the ice retreated, the land rebounded slowly, in places as much as 500', and cut off access to the sea. This allowed the Champlain Basin to fill with fresh water. Rebound is still occurring and eventually the north end of Lake Champlain may rise enough to block drainage from the Richeau River. Some geologists believe Lake Champlain once again may drain to the south via the Hudson.

While the Champlain Basin still was connected to the ocean via the Champlain Sea, Atlantic salmon were able to establish themselves in the rivers draining into the Champlain Basin. When the ocean waters retreated, these fish adapted to fresh water and now utilize Lake Champlain as their "sea." Today we know them as the landlocked salmon so highly prized by fishermen.

Yet another glacial feature, relatively rare in the Adirondacks, is the *cirque*. High on the slopes of some prominent peaks are small, hollow depressions that look as if someone has taken a giant ice cream scoop to the mountainsides. These examples of glacial scour-power were formed after the great ice sheets had retreated, but while it was still cold and snowy enough for smaller glaciers to form at high elevations. These small pockets of glacial ice began to move downslope, plucking rock away from the backs of the basins. This action, repeated time and again, created the bowl-like hollows we call cirques. One of the most visible Adirondack cirques is located on the west side of Giant Mountain above Roaring Brook. Other cirques can be seen on Whiteface Mountain, Big Slide Mountain, Cascade Mountain and Mount Dix.

Above: *Lake Champlain, sixth largest freshwater lake in the United States, forms the border between Vermont and New York. The lake basin once was occupied by an immense glacier. So great was the weight of this ice that it actually depressed the earth's surface and, once the glacier melted, underlying rocks began to rebound. Since the end of the ice age the Lake Champlain basin has risen hundreds of feet.*
Facing page: *The rocks exposed in the High Peaks region are a metamorphic rock known as anorthosite. Gradually uplifted, the overlying younger sedimentary rocks that once covered it were eroded away.*
GEORGE WUERTHNER PHOTOS

High on the slopes of some prominent peaks are small, hollow depressions that look as if someone has taken a giant ice cream scoop to the mountainsides.

The geological picture of the Adirondacks is like a puzzle with some of the pieces still missing.

Above: Glacial lakes once covered the valleys along the road to Adirondak Loj. Glacial silt settling out of the water created good agricultural lands, such as the South Meadows pictured here.
Right: Looking to Mt. Marcy from Mt. Algonquin in the High Peaks. The streaks of bare rock on Mt. Colden in the middle distance were created by landslides. The underlying basement rock is so smooth that saturated soils on steep slopes sometimes will peel away, exposing the bare rock beneath.
GEORGE WUERTHNER PHOTOS

WEATHERING

Although the Ice Age glaciers left the greatest imprint upon the Adirondack Mountains, many other natural forces have been working on these mountains for eons, and some are locally prominent. For example, the constant freezing and thawing of ice locked in tiny cracks and along joints in the bedrock slowly breaks apart the rock. On a steep slope, this broken material will tumble down; repeated over and over, the process eventually forms a hillside of rubble hikers know as a *talus slope.*

Exfoliation is another weathering process commonly seen in the Adirondacks. Exfoliation results when rock formed deep in the earth under stupendous pressure is gradually exhumed. Relieved of the overlying burden and pressure, the rock expands and cracks, resulting in the peeling away of shell-like slabs of rock. One of the most famous examples of exfoliation in the United State is Half Dome in Yosemite National Park, but similar formations can be found throughout the Adirondacks' High Peaks region.

Slide strips are another Adirondack geologic feature common on the higher peaks. These originate on steep, smooth slopes composed of anorthosite bedrock. Topsoil and vegetation have a difficult time gaining a foothold on such featureless rock. If saturated by excessive rain or spring thaws, the soil peels away in a massive landslide, creating the stripes so prominent on peaks like Giant Mountain, Mount Colden, Haystack Mountain and others.

The geological picture of the Adirondacks is like a puzzle with some of the pieces still missing. No one has an entirely clear idea of the final images, but each year new parts are fitted into place, and gradually the picture becomes clearer and sharper. Nevertheless, there always will be some room for new interpretation and new insights, which will keep the science of geology forever young and interesting, and continue to provide lovers of Adirondack lore something new and fresh to discover.

BOGS

A legacy of the Ice Age and one of the most interesting plant communities found in the Adirondacks is the bog. Bogs occupy depressions or old lake beds originally created by the retreating glaciers. Most of the meadow-like, open areas surrounded by stunted trees that one sees in the Adirondacks are bogs. In many cases, the mat of vegetation seen along the edges and towards the centers of a bog is merely floating on water. This mat can be so thick that it's possible to walk on it, although it will quiver like a bowl of gelatin.

Bogs form when decaying vegetation depletes oxygen levels of poorly drained basins. Without oxygen, organisms like bacteria, which are responsible for organic breakdown, can no longer survive. Decomposition grinds to a snail's pace and a bog is born. Whatever dies in these highly acidic, oxygen-poor waters is "mummified," as the several-thousand-year-old bodies found in northern European bogs attest.

With decay almost non-existent, organic matter gradually accumulates, building up layer after layer, to form peat. One of the most common plants contributing to the formation of peat is sphagnum moss, a chief component of the floating-mat plant community typical of bogs. Sphagnum moss is composed of dead subsurface water-storage cells and living surface ones that produce food. If you pick up a hand full of sphagnum and squeeze it, water will pour from it like a sponge. So absorbent is it, that Indians used sphagnum moss for baby diapers.

Because of the acidity and the generally cold conditions of the watery environment, breakdown of organic matter is exceedingly slow. Nutrients necessary for plant growth are locked in the undecayed matter, hence many bog plants (such as the black spruce) are adapted to living in a nutrient-poor environment. Other typical bog plants, like the pitcher plant and sundew, are carnivorous and obtain scarce nutrients like nitrogen by capturing and eating insects.

The pitcher plant, with its large vase-shaped leaves, probably is the most specialized in this regard. An odor attracts insect victims inside the plant's opening. If they venture down the plant's throat, downward-pointing spines prevent their escape. The slippery interior causes victims to slide into a pool at the bottom, where digestive enzymes immediately begin dissolving the body.

Another level of life is found within the pitcher plant. A flesh fly, *Sacrophaga sarraceniae,* lays its eggs within the pitcher plant's liquid. Once the eggs hatch, the fly's larvae or maggots live upon other insects that happen to fall into the plant's liquid. For some unexplained reason, the maggots themselves are unaffected by the digestive enzymes.

Many bog plants also are adapted to a life of water deprivation. It may sound strange considering most mat vegetation rests upon water, but the roots of many plants growing on top never contact the underlying water layer. Bog plants like Labrador tea, cranberry, leatherleaf and others have thick leaves that retard water losses.

Over a long enough period of time, the accumulating mass of dead vegetation will completely fill in a basin. The bog will be transformed into a wet meadow and eventually into a forest.

Saranac Lake Wild Forest.
GEORGE WUERTHNER

The Adirondack bog not only is a special place for plants and animals, but also it often provides the only natural openings other than lakes within an otherwise solid forest covering. It is an important scenic attribute of the Adirondack region.

VEGETATION

Because of changes associated with elevation gain, as well as differences in soil characteristics resulting from geological and biological history, the Adirondacks display a relatively wide variety of plant communities, considering their relatively northern location.

VEGETATIVE ZONES

As a general rule, hardwoods in the Adirondacks occupy the better-drained sites and more productive soils while conifers tend to dominate the harsher growing sites near timberline, in nutrient-poor soils, in excessively wet or extremely droughty soils.

Elevation and soil productivity are the main determinants and, consequently, a predictable series of plant community zones is encountered as one moves from wetlands to well drained sites, and from lowlands up to the highest peaks. Every 1,000' gain in elevation represents a climatic change equivalent to moving 300 miles farther north. Any plant living atop Mt. Marcy must endure environmental conditions very similar to those found along the Arctic Ocean, and indeed many plant species found there are merely arctic species that had moved south during the Ice Age and were isolated on high Adirondack peaks after the glaciers' retreat.

On the poorly drained low-elevation sites, the plant association usually referred to as the bog community survives stagnant, acidic, nutrient-poor water, hence environments. A dominant bog plant is sphagnum moss, which tolerates these acidic waters and frequently forms floating mats of vegetation along the shores of shallow lakes.

At the edge of the bog grows black spruce, a species that tolerates waterlogged soils and is specifically adapted to sites low in available nutrients. Mixed in with black spruce you often will find another coniferous species, tamarack.

As you move toward higher, better-drained ground, you reach a transition zone where hardwoods such as red maple and yellow birch, along with conifers like white pine, begin to replace the species indicative of bog habitats. This transition zone eventually gives way to the dominant Adirondack forest type—the northern hardwood forest composed of sugar maple, American beech and yellow birch with lesser amounts of such conifers as eastern hemlock and white pine.

Every 1,000' gain in elevation represents a climatic change equivalent to moving 300 miles farther north.

Left: *Dwarf dogwood on Mt. Marcy.*

Facing page: *Balsam fir at timberline on Mt. Marcy assumes a low, stunted position covered by snow. Blasting winds kill any branches that stick up above the snow, thus shearing trees to dwarf condition.*
GEORGE WUERTHNER PHOTOS

25

At higher elevations climatic conditions are colder and harsher, resulting once again in slower decomposition and limited nutrients. Because of increasingly difficult growing conditions, a marked change takes place in forest composition at about 2,500′ where hardwoods largely are replaced by a coniferous forest known as the boreal forest or spruce-fir zone for its two major components: red spruce and balsam fir. Although hardwoods can usually overwhelm conifers on the better soils and under moderate climatic conditions, they are not so well suited for growth where nutrients are limited or soils are marked by drought or excessive moisture. Under these environmental constraints, the conifers dominate.

Near the limits of tree growth, called timberline, red spruce fades and pure balsam fir forests dominate what is sometimes called the subalpine zone. Under the extremely stressful conditions found at these higher elevations—short growing season, high wind, and cold temperatures—the fir takes a stunted form, often growing no taller than an average man. Here trees utilize every depression and boulder for shelter from the fierce winds, and sprawl in low twisted forms called krummholz, which means "crooked stick" in German.

At these higher elevations, snow is often an ally of the plants, blanketing them in winter with a protective sheathing that prevents water loss, reduces wind abrasion damage, and moderates temperature extremes. Frequent sights near timberline are the dead and abraded tops of trees, which indicate the average snow depth. Below the snow the growing plant has been protected, while stems that stick up above this level are sheared off by the wind.

Above: Red spruce is one of the major components of the boreal forest that typically occupies areas above 2,500′ elevation in the Adirondacks. It is particularly sensitive to acid rain and studies show major die-offs of mature spruce in many areas of the park. ***Top right:*** Abundant rainfall supports the lush growth of ferns along the Ausable River. GEORGE WUERTHNER PHOTOS

LOGGING

In the 1800s wood meant wealth. Houses and wagons were made of wood; the fuel used to heat and cook was wood. In the Adirondacks even many of the roads were built from wooden planks to cover the wet and muddy segments. In many eastern cities wood was scarce and expensive. It might require one tenth of an individual's daily wages to buy wood to cook one meal. In Europe, where the forests had been cut for centuries, the shortage of forests created an even greater demand.

Despite the value of wood in the cities on the frontier, wood was wasted on a scale that would bring condemnation today. To the early farmers who sought to wrestle a living from the land, trees were merely an encumbrance that hid the soil and needed to be cleared.

But the growing national and international appetite for wood soon made New York State a major lumbering state. By 1813, the sounds of logging could be heard along the Schroon River and, before long, Glen Falls on the Hudson became a major mill town with timber fed to it by a dozen Adirondack waterways. By 1850, New York surpassed Maine as the largest producer of timber, with some 1.6 billion board feet cut annually.

At first, nearly all the logging was focused on white pines. As a softwood it floated well, and without a railroad or road network, log drives on the river provided the only feasible means of moving logs from the woods to the mills. In colonial times, white pine was particularly abundant in the Lake Champlain–Lake George region. Even today white pine dominates this region, making up 20 percent of the forests here.

The cutting of pine and later other species was done in autumn, and logs were sledded out of the woods in winter after the snow fell. Many loggers were farmers in the summer months and available for logging only after the crops had been harvested. In addition, in the days before practical road construction, it was easier to use the frozen ground for a highway, than to negotiate the often-muddy morass that would develop in summer.

Lumberjacks worked all fall cutting the timber. Then the logs were dragged by oxen to a central loading area. Once snow fell and winter began, the logs were loaded on

White pines were the first species to be cut, in the 1830s. Pharaoh Lake Wilderness. GEORGE WUERTHNER

Above: Fresh snow on red pines in the McKenzie Mountain Wilderness.
Right: The evergreen balsam fir (right center), along with red spruce, became one of the major pulp trees beginning in the mid-1800s. GEORGE WUERTHNER PHOTOS

by a team of horses over a frozen winter road. On steep hills straw gave the horses surer traction, while on the flat ground the surface was iced to ease sledding. The greatest fear of the teamster was to lose control of the sled on a downhill slope for the sled sometimes raced like a toboggan. Many drivers and their teams were injured or crushed to death by runaway log sleds.

Teamsters hauled the logs to a frozen river or lake called the banking ground, where the timber was unloaded onto the ice to await break-up in the spring, when it was hoped that high water would carry the logs downstream to the mills. If a log did not get caught in a jam, it could travel from Newcomb to Glens Falls in about two days.

Dams were constructed in some headwater streams to back up additional water. These later were dynamited to create a virtual wall of water that would transport the timber out of the mountains. Other dams were constructed to flood lowlands, thereby connecting a string of lakes to form a continuous waterway suitable for rafting logs. These were called "flows" and are a common legacy of the early logging days in the Adirondacks.

One of the most prestigious as well as dangerous jobs was that of log driver. A driver rode the floating logs downstream, freeing jams or pile-ups with an iron-tipped pole. Many of these log drivers could not swim and merely slipping off a log meant death in the frigid northern waters. Beyond that, the logs constantly jostled each other and occasionally piled up, often throwing the unfortunate driver into the mass of rapidly-moving, colliding trees where he would be crushed.

When a log jam developed, the driver had to walk toward the middle of the pile-up attempting to locate what was known as the key log. This was a very dangerous operation since, once loosened, the jam would often break up with an explosive surge, sending logs flying through the air. The driver had to be quick on his feet to avoid being tossed into the river before the oncoming logs.

Log drivers also chased logs in a special craft called a "jam" boat. The boat usually held three men, one to row plus two others who poked at the logs to break apart log jams and in other ways kept the timber moving toward the mills. Although this was not quite so dangerous as riding the logs, many boats

were capsized or crushed if caught in the midst of the torrent of logs.

There were no holidays on a log drive, for the timber had to be kept moving toward the mill. Working seven days a week, dawn to dusk, soaked to the skin by frigid spring-time waters, left many a man crippled with rheumatism before he was 40.

Since big rivers like the Hudson might be used by dozens of logging companies during the spring drive season, each log was branded so that its owner could be identified once it arrived at a large bend near Glen Falls. It served as a natural corral known as the "big boom," where logs were collected and sorted. Companies often cooperated on the costs of a drive and wrote contracts explaining the exact obligations of each crew.

The last log drive on the Hudson took place in 1924, and logs still were being sent down the Moose River as late as 1948. But the establishment of paved highways and logging trucks made log driving obsolete.

And with it passed the old-time logging camp. Since most of the cutting was done in remote locations and roads were nonexistent, lumberjacks had to live at forest camps located next to the

logging area. Each camp had between 15 and 45 men, and a few women who served as cooks. The usual fare was salt pork, bread, beans, hotcakes, eggs and gallons of coffee—all served in amazing quantities. Little cooking

shanties followed the men down river much like the western chuck wagons providing the men with hot food as the drive progressed. In looking at old photos of the logging camp inhabitants, it becomes apparent that most

An old logging tractor skidder rusts away where it was abandoned in the Five Ponds Wilderness.
GEORGE WUERTHNER

Many of the large fires near the turn of the century had their origins with trains that lumbermen used to remove trees. Due to fires, paper birch (pictured here) came to dominate much of the forest.
TOM TILL

lumberjacks were young men, for few could survive the extremely difficult working conditions and the isolation.

Although the original Adirondack logging industry selectively harvested white pine, by 1840 the large old eastern hemlocks began to be cut and stripped of their bark for the leather tanning industry. Since hemlock wood was considered inferior as lumber, loggers usually took only the bark and the rest of the tree was left behind as slash. By 1840, more than 270 tanneries were located in or near the Adirondacks and the harvest of hemlocks was heavy, almost wiping out the species in these mountains.

About the time loggers nearly exhausted the Adiron- dacks' supply of white pine, there was another change in the forest products industry: the sulfite paper process. Wood pulp rapidly replaced rags in paper manu- facture, and the first pulp paper mill was built on the Hudson in 1866. By 1890, New York led the country in pulp manufacturing. The preferred species was red spruce, although balsam fir also could be used. By 1899 more than 200 mil- lion board feet of spruce pulp was being cut each year in the Adirondacks. Since pulp could be made from almost any size log, cutting for pulp made selec- tive harvesting obsolete and the common practice became clearcutting.

As a result of logging and land clearing for farming, by 1880 only 25 percent of New York state was still forested. (Today 61 percent is tree covered). In 1885, it was estimated that at least two thirds of the Adirondack forest had been cut over once, and this was before the peak in pulp production. Rapid deforestation in the Adirondacks began to worry many observers. The denuded slopes eroded quickly and, without the shade provided by forest cover, winter snow melted quickly—increasing downstream flooding and aggravating summer droughts. The use of rivers for log drives and the torrents released by splash dams wrought havoc with the fisheries. Finally, the logging practices of the day left behind tons of slash, which often caught fire. Sparks from the coal-fired trains used to haul logs out of the mountains often were the ignition source. In the worst two years, 1903 and 1908, a total of 464,000 acres and 368,000 acres respectively were consumed. Of the 377 fires investigated in 1903, a total of 121 were started by trains.

Above: *The typical mid-elevation Adirondack forest is a mixture of evergreen species including white pine, red spruce and balsam fir, along with sugar maple, yellow birch and American beech. Seen here is the Sargent Ponds Wild Forest.*

Right: *In autumn, the cold-sensitive leaf pigment, chlorophyll, breaks down, allowing the yellows and oranges of carotenoid pigments and red and purple of anthocyanins, previously masked by chlorophyll, to be seen. Maple leaves, Five Ponds Wilderness.*

The occurrence of each individual species is not a result of random distribution, but depends a great deal upon ecological tolerance and strategy.

31

At the very upper limits of tree growth, particularly where soils are extremely shallow and wet, balsam fir may give way to black spruce, which seems to find its niche where no other tree can grow—at timberline and in bogs.

But there are limits even to where black spruce can grow. Trees require a minimum of two months when the average temperature is 50 degrees or higher. On the highest Adirondack peaks, this requirement is not met, and trees are replaced by alpine tundra characterized by low, mat-like "cushion" plants. Only 11 Adirondack peaks have any alpine tundra at all and the aggregate acreage amounts to little more than 80 acres. By comparison, the slightly higher White Mountains in New Hampshire have nearly 5,000 acres of alpine tundra.

ADIRONDACK TREE SPECIES

As can be seen, the occurrence of each individual species is not a result of random distribution, but depends a great deal upon ecological tolerance and strategy. Ecological tolerance is the sum total of a species' environmental requirements and how well that plant can cope with environmental pressures. Some species, paper birch for example, require full sunlight for successful germination and growth. These species, called pioneer species, tend to invade and rapidly colonize disturbed sites such as recent burns or areas abandoned after logging operations. But their own seedlings cannot grow in the shade of the parents, so pioneer species gradually disappear as the forest canopy closes over. At the other extreme are climax tree species which can tolerate—or even require—shady conditions and can grow well even in competition with other species. Eastern hemlock, a tree common to shaded, mossy glens, is one such species.

No plant is perfectly adapted for widely divergent environmental conditions, hence certain species tend to defeat other species under a given set of conditions. Some species are highly specialized for their environments, such as the alpine plants that grow atop the highest Adirondack peaks, while other species like red maple seem able to grow in a wide variety of habitats, but never dominate any.

Black spruce

Black spruce has a number of adaptations that give it a competitive edge in one of its preferred habitats: bogs. These include a shallow root system that enables the spruce to colonize surfaces lacking any real soil development, an ability to survive on low-productivity soils where biological decomposition is slow; and a tolerance for having its roots submerged all or some of the time. Thus the ecological strategy of the black spruce is to avoid competition by growing in environments where other species cannot survive.

Because of the difficult growing environment typical of most of its habitat, a mature black spruce may go years between good seed crops—if it produces any seeds at all. In addition, seedlings have a difficult time getting established under the hostile growing regime. As compensation, black spruce is able to reproduce vegetatively by a process called layering. On extremely harsh sites, such as the snowy environment at timberline, the lower branches may be pushed down to the soil by heavy snowfall. Occasionally one of these branches will establish a new root system and become a genetic clone of the parent plant.

Vegetative reproduction is a common ecological strategy for species that inhabit inhospitable growing sites, but it has its drawbacks. For example, no genetic material is exchanged and this limits a species' ability to adapt to new environmental stresses. This works in environments where there is little competition from other species, but it's a handicap under most growing conditions.

Tamarack

Tamarack often is an associate of black spruce, growing in wet, open locations, where it often forms pure stands. Like black spruce, it can tolerate having its roots submerged in stagnant, frigid water, and thus commonly grows upon the floating mats that fringe many bogs. Despite these similarities to the black spruce, the tamarack exemplifies a slightly different approach to the same environmental stresses.

Although the tamarack is a conifer or cone-bearing tree, it is not evergreen. Instead, its needles turn a brilliant gold in autumn and then are shed for the winter. Without needles, the tamarack is less susceptible than black spruce to wind shear, water losses and branch breakage due to snow accumulations than black spruce. But these advantages come at a cost. While conifers like black spruce photosynthesize during the winter and spring months whenever temperatures rise to near or above freezing, tamarack is dormant and misses these opportunities to manufacture additional energy. It must do all its photosynthesis, and hence its yearly growth, during a very short summer season. Because of the tamarack's limited leaf area, it grows well only where it has full access to sunlight

(such as in the open bog), but it does poorly if shaded, so one seldom finds it growing in the gloom of a closed-canopy forest.

Despite this limitation, tamarack survives well because of the limited competition from other trees in swamps and bog. It can afford to grow slowly, and does not produce its first cones until 50 or 75 years old. But on more productive sites, the tamarack's slow growth and its light requirements are major disadvantages. In growth strategies, the tamarack is the proverbial turtle: on better soils the tactic fails when tamaracks compete with species that can establish themselves quickly, particularly on recently disturbed sites, and then mature rapidly. This latter strategy is more like the hare's than the turtle's approach in the race for survival, and paper birch exemplifies this tactic well.

Paper birch

Paper birch, one of the easiest trees to identify because its peeling white bark resembles parchment, invades disturbed sites such as those recently burned by fire, hence is often referred to as a pioneering species. Once established, paper birch grows quickly, overtopping its competition and maturing rapidly—often producing seeds within 15 years of

Above: Tamarack, or eastern larch, is a deciduous conifer. In autumn its needles turn golden and are shed. It usually is found in open bog areas.
Facing page: Large forest fires burned much of the High Peaks region near the turn of the century. Paper birch, a fast-growing pioneer species of recently burned areas, came to dominate much of the forest in this region. Gradually, the sunlight-dependent birch was replaced by shade-tolerant evergreen species like red spruce and balsam fir. Here, red spruce are beginning to overtake the paper birch.
Inset: Sorrel and ferns grow on the nearly shrubless floor beneath a red spruce forest. West Canada Lakes Wilderness.
GEORGE WUERTHNER PHOTOS

33

establishment. These seeds are shed during the fall and winter months when storms are prevalent, thus ensuring wide distribution. It does not take long for birch to dominate a site, as the nearly pure stands visible along the Cascade Lakes attest.

Aspen

Aspen is another common pioneering Adirondack species, but it utilizes a different method for rapid colonization and dominance of a disturbed site. Although a lavish seed producer, its germination and seedling survival rate is poor. Instead, most aspen reproduction is by root suckers. When the aboveground stems are destroyed, aspen will sprout new shoots from its roots. As many as 60,000 suckers per acre may be produced following some catastrophe like fire, hence aspen is sometimes termed a "weed" species.

Yellow birch

Contrasting with these aggressive strategies, of aspen and paper birch, trees like yellow birch have adapted to a different environment—the maturing forest. Unlike pioneer species, yellow birch is shade-tolerant; it can live and reproduce in the shade of a forest canopy. The yellow birch does not depend upon an environment that is transient in nature and thus it can afford to develop and mature at a more leisurely pace—often not producing its first seeds until 35 to 40 years old.

Unlike pioneering species that tend to grow in nearly pure, single-species stands, yellow birch usually is associated with other tree species. Yet, it is a very distinctive tree in the mature Adirondack forest because it attains massive proportions—at least for these cut-over forests—with trunks of up to four feet in diameter and heights of 100' allowing it to tower over all other hardwood species. Only the eastern white pine, a conifer, grows taller here. Individual yellow birches have been known to live for more than 200 years—and even after death the shaggy barked giants survive for years as snags, serving as veritable apartment buildings for a host of cavity-dependent wildlife species like pileated woodpeckers and flying squirrels.

Sugar maple

If left undisturbed, a forest eventually progresses toward a climax condition where only species even more shade-tolerant than the yellow birch can survive. In the Adirondacks, the tree that fills this role more than any other

Above: The boreal forest, typically found across Canada and north to Alaska, reaches its southern limits in the Adirondack Park. This is along the South Branch of the Grass River.
Right: The peeling white bark of paper birch was used by Indians to construct canoes. It also is extremely flammable, and may actually invite fires, since, as a shade-intolerant species, it usually replaces itself after fire has created sunlight and bare mineral soil the birch needs for successful regeneration.
GEORGE WUERTHNER PHOTOS
Facing page: Sugar maple and American beech along the Ausable River. JAMES RANDKLEV

is the sugar maple—the state tree of New York. Its ecological strategy is to out-live the competition. If suppressed by the shade of taller trees, sugar maple saplings survive for years, barely adding new growth, waiting for an opening in the canopy, which once found allows it to grow quickly, surging upward toward the light to become one of the dominant forest trees.

Because it is a long-lived species (up to 350 years) that grows well in shade, sugar maple is one of the most widespread and numerous species in the Adirondacks. If no disturbance occurs in the forest, chances are good that, after 100 years or so, the site will be dominated by sugar maple—assuming the species can establish itself there in the first place. With the legal protection enjoyed by the Adirondack Park, it can be expected that sugar maple will likely comprise an even greater proportion of the Adirondack forest than at present.

American beech

Often found growing in association with the sugar maple is another shade-tolerant climax species—American beech. Beech is found in a wide variety of sites, but does best on well drained soils and will not grow on poorly drained sites such as bogs and swamps. The easiest time of year to identify beech is winter because, unlike most deciduous trees whose leaves drop from the tree with autumn, the smooth gray-barked beech has a habit of retaining many dried leaves throughout the winter, particularly on smaller trees.

The overall percentage of American beech in the Adirondack forest has been increasing since the 1800s, because the tree is not considered suitable for timber harvest. Loggers leave it behind while removing more valuable species like white pine and sugar maple. Beech, like aspen, sprouts from suckers, thus enabling it to take advantage of any openings created by logging operations or natural disturbance.

Although not suitable for wood products, beech nevertheless serves an important ecological function since its large, oily fruit, the beech nut, is an important food for many wildlife species including deer, bear, squirrels, grouse, and turkey.

Eastern hemlock

One of the longest-lived Adirondack species is the eastern hemlock, which may survive for as many as 600 years. As might be expected with a species of this longevity, it will reach massive proportions, but throughout the Adirondack

region, such large trees are extremely rare. Hemlock bark once was used in leather tanning, and many of the ancient trees were felled and stripped of their bark to supply the tanneries common all along the fringes of the Adirondacks during the late 1800s.

Furthermore, hemlock is excellent deer forage. Although there always were some deer in the Adirondack region, the herds really boomed after logging opened up the forest canopy, creating many shrubby hardwood sites where food was readily available. As a result the herds increased, and

As many as 60,000 aspen suckers per acre may be produced following some catastrophe like fire, hence the tree is sometimes termed a "weed" species.

35

Eastern hemlock, seen here, is the longest-lived Adirondack tree species, attaining ages of as much as 600 years. In the 1800s, many hemlocks were cut and stripped of their bark, which is high in tannin, a major ingredient for tanning leather. JAMES RANDKLEV

Some pines were said to be more than 200' in height and as much as six feet in diameter.

expanded into regions where they otherwise were scarce. Increasingly, they turned to hemlock for their winter food, and in many places eliminated nearly all the young hemlock trees. This may not pose a serious problem for the long-lived hemlock. It needs only 20 to 30 years free of heavy deer browsing for new seedlings to become established and to grow beyond the reach of deer, thus ensuring its long-term continuity in the Adirondack flora.

White pine

Another prominent Adirondack forest species is the eastern white pine. Prior to the logging era, immense white pine forests dominated the slopes of Lake Champlain and Lake George and were found scattered elsewhere throughout the Adirondack region. Some of these pines were said to be more than 200' in height and as much as six feet in diameter. They were extremely valuable for their clear, smooth grain and easily worked wood. In the days of sailing ships, the tall trunks often were used for masts.

Although the loggers went through the Adirondacks cutting most of the mature white pine, the species is exceedingly aggressive and readily colonizes open areas, such as abandoned farm fields or openings in the forest. Once established, white pine quickly outgrows its hardwood competition, so it's not uncommon to see white pine above the surrounding forest canopy. It is also drought-tolerant because it has a long tap root, which allows it to reach water beyond the reach of other plants. It grows on very well drained sites, like sandy eskers, where other trees would die from dehydration.

The white pine easily is one of the most majestic Adirondack trees, particularly where one encounters remnant old-growth stands missed by early-day loggers. One can get an idea of the original Adirondack forest in Five Ponds Wilderness, where there are towering individual white pines as well as small groves that were bypassed by the loggers.

Although this chapter has dealt primarily dealt with trees, the ecological principles apply equally well to other plants including lichens, mosses, flowers and shrubs. Each plant has specific ecological needs and tolerances, and it has evolved strategies that enable it to survive under some, but not all, circumstances.

ALPINE TUNDRA

The plant community type most rare in the Adirondacks is alpine tundra. Tundra is recorded for only 11 peaks and covers no more than 80 acres. More than half of this total is found on two peaks, Algonquin and Marcy, but Wright, Iroquois, Skylight, Haystack, Dix, Basin, Gothics and Colden all have small patches of this unique community. Whiteface Mountain once had a smattering of tundra, but the construction of buildings, and roads to its summit, compromised the ecological integrity of this alpine region.

Many of the plant species growing on these higher peaks are identical or similar to species found in the Arctic several thousand miles farther north. Isolated to the highest summits by changing climatic conditions after the retreat of the Ice Age glaciers, these plants inhabit a life zone no different from that found next to the Arctic Ocean. Although alpine plant communities often are composed of species slightly different from those found in the Arctic, they nevertheless share an ability to live and prosper under environmental conditions most other plants find inhospitable and impossible to endure. For example, weather information collected on Whiteface Mountain indicates that the average temperature is 10° to 15° cooler than in surrounding lowlands, wind speeds *average* 35 mph, and moisture and cloud cover are markedly higher than at lower elevations. All this translates into a harsher environment with a growing season of two months or less.

Some of the plants found on Adirondack summits are merely lowland bog species that have moved upslope. For example, sphagnum moss, Labrador tea and leatherleaf all are common bog plants also found in the alpine community. Many characteristics of bogs are similar to conditions found

High winds seen here flailing at alpine vegetation atop Mt. Marcy are a factor in creating alpine tundra. This extremely fragile and rare plant community is found on only 11 peaks and occupies about 80 acres.
GEORGE WUERTHNER

Blueberry, deer hair and lichens growing at 4,700' between Algonquin and Boundary mountains. K.A. WILSON

on high peaks, namely few available nutrients, and cold, acidic, water-logged soils.

Other plants, such as *Diapensia* and alpine bilberry, are restricted to the alpine tundra regions of the Adirondacks.

No matter where else they may or may not grow, all alpine plants exhibit a few basic adaptations to their rugged environment. Most alpine plants tend to be perennial—that is they survive more than a single season. In fact, for many of these hardy mountain dwellers, it takes years of slow growth just to save enough energy for a single season of flowering. That flower you see among the alpine cushions may be the accumulated growth of up to 10 seasons.

Alpine plants tend to be small, occupying depressions or growing in mat-like forms close to the ground. This lifeform has several advantages. It allows the plant to use less energy to grow their aboveground structures of leaves, stems and branches by avoiding the worst buffetings of the often hurricane-force gales that surround the peaks.

Many alpine plants have large root systems in proportion to their aboveground structures,

although their flowering structures also may be quite large in proportion to their stems and leaves. There are several reasons for this division of resources. Because of the very short growing season available to alpine plants, they must begin flowering as soon as snow cover disappears in the spring. This is often before it's warm enough for maximum photosynthesis, so a plant must live off the energy stored from previous seasons of growth. Most of this excess energy is stored in below-ground structures like roots.

In addition, in the treeless alpine environment a plant does not need to be tall to avoid shading, hence alpine plants can reduce the percentage of aboveground structures like stalks and stems and allot a greater percentage of their limited energy to root-system development. A massive root system also gives these plants a firm anchor to the windswept slope.

During many summers, conditions are less than suitable for successful flowering, germination and establishment of seedlings. It becomes important to many species that they survive more than a single season so as to increase their chances of successful reproduction

during the infrequent summers when conditions are favorable.

Many alpine plants are evergreen, thus saving them energy necessary for a yearly replacement of leaves. In addition, evergreen species have a jump over deciduous plants when it comes to photosynthesis since they can begin manufacturing energy immediately in the spring while deciduous species first must grow leaves.

Plants with evergreen leaves, like alpine bilberry and leatherleaf, have another adaptive advantage—they are efficient at water retention. The thick, often waxy, cuticle or outer layer of the leaf protects the inner portion from rapid water loss. In the windy alpine environment, particularly in rocky locations, water loss can be substantial. Winter is a particularly dangerous time, since plants still may transpire water, but replacing it may be impossible if the ground is frozen.

Alpine plants reproduce in a number of ways. Some, such as grasses and sedges, often propagate by rhizomes, or runners, which are underground stems that send up new shoots. The new plant is still attached to its parent root system, and thus can survive periods of

adversity that might kill independent young plants.

Those plants that rely exclusively upon flowers for reproduction disperse their seeds by several methods. Some produce light seeds that are released to the wind. In the alpine environment, there usually is no shortage of gales to spread seeds far and wide. Other plants produce far fewer seeds, which are larger and heavier. These tend to be contained in dry capsules elevated above the normal snow height. During winter storms these capsules rattle and shake and the seeds are tossed out to be blown across the snow cover. With luck, their new location may be suitable for successful germination.

Due to the fragility and scarcity of Adirondack alpine terrains, and their locations on the highest treeless peaks (also the most popular hiking destinations within the park), the tundra has been severely impacted in a number of locations. Once the vegetation dies, the wind and rain often scour the soil down to bare rock. It will take literally thousands of years to be replaced.

Timberline on Mt. Algonquin. Dwarf trees grade into alpine tundra on the highest peaks. Trees need a minimum of two months where the temperature averages more than 50°F.
GEORGE WUERTHNER

39

WILDLIFE

3

Moose are the largest member of the deer family and once were found throughout the Adirondacks. Extirpated by 1861 with the last documented animal killed near Raquette Lake, moose are drifting into the Adirondacks from Vermont and may number anywhere between 30 and 60 animals at this time.

GEORGE WUERTHNER

The story of Adirondack wildlife parallels that of almost every part of the country: abundance, then reckless exploitation, followed by regulation and protection that in some cases halted the decline of species. For some animals here, the regulations came too late.

The Adirondack region never was as productive wildlife habitat as lower-elevation areas outside the mountains. Although various Indian tribes occasionally entered the Adirondacks to hunt, no tribe actually lived in these mountains. There were better hunting, fishing and farming elsewhere. It is only because most of the lower-elevation wildlife habitat has been transformed into housing developments, farmlands and shopping malls that the Adirondacks have a reputation today as a place to hunt, fish or just enjoy wildlife.

EXPLOITATION

The first destructive exploitation of Adirondack wildlife came even before the first white settlers invaded the mountains. Not long after Samuel Champlain left the lake that now bears his name, French traders operating along the St. Lawrence River and Dutch traders with forts along the Hudson had begun exchanging European goods with local Indians for furs. In their quest for pelts, Indians moved their traplines farther and farther afield, eventually tapping the Adirondack region. Then, as now, it was rich habitat for furbearers like the beaver. By the late 1700s or early 1800s at the latest, Indian trapping had eliminated or severely depressed beaver populations over much of New York, including the Adirondacks.

By the early 1800s, with better lands to the south already taken, settlers began to move into the fringes of the mountains. Although New York had passed a law in 1705 regulating the taking of deer, little effort was made at its enforcement, especially in more remote portions of the state. Most frontier families considered unlimited harvesting of

game a personal right, and they regularly ignored any restrictions to hunting or fishing. In addition, most settlers viewed predators as a threat to their livestock and to the deer they themselves wanted to hunt, thus wolves, mountain lions and wolverines soon disappeared before the onslaught of traps, poison and guns.

By the turn of the century, the woods were empty of many species that once had been common in these

Ringneck snakes are common under logs in the deciduous forest.
JOHN SERRAO

41

mountains. The last moose was shot at Raquette Lake in 1861; the last mountain lion by 1894. No one seems to know exactly when the last wolf was killed, but the last bounty was paid in 1899 in St. Lawrence County. Other species that have disappeared as breeding populations include the lynx and wolverine. Other species disappeared not so much because of direct persecution, but rather from habitat changes or indirect poisoning from pesticides in their food chains. The list of such species includes golden and bald eagles, peregrine falcons, spruce grouse and ravens. Even species that are today widely distributed and common, such as whitetail deer, once were near extinction over much of the Adirondacks because of the uncontrolled hunting of the 1800s.

RECOVERY

Although the original purpose for setting up the Adirondack Forest Preserve was to protect watersheds, another benefit has been the preservation of wildlife habitat. This protection, coupled with stricter enforcement of fish and game regulations along with a better understanding of wildlife needs, has resulted in the recovery of many species.

Whitetail deer

Perhaps the best example of a species that recovered well as a result of the combination of these protective measures is the whitetail deer, which are extremely adaptive to human influences and tolerate many kinds of intrusions except the elimination of prime winter ranges. The deer can thrive in the presence of humans because it is a species adapted to edges. It does best on habitats that have openings mixed with cover. After settlers opened the forest canopy by logging, farming and mining, deer habitat increased, and deer populations boomed.

Deer are prolific breeders and each doe normally produces two fawns a year; in better habitats populations can be expected to increase by 40 percent each spring. Once all predators except humans were eliminated, deer were free to breed themselves out of their food supply, and nearly did so by the 1960s. Despite hunting, many herds continued to grow until they were knocked down by a hard winter as thousands starved or died from malnutrition.

To decrease a deer herd, game managers reduce the number of breeding females; the institution of doe seasons is one way to accomplish this goal. If range conditions are good,

By the turn of the century, the woods were empty of many species that once had been common in these mountains.

regulated deer hunting will have little long-term impact. If deer herds are not reduced by hunting, nature eventually does the reduction through range deterioration and starvation, but not until the winter range has been destroyed. Some uninformed hunters complain that doe seasons will "ruin" deer hunting. In some years, it is quite likely that hunters may kill more deer than necessary to maintain habitat quality, but it is much better to harvest a few extra animals than to allow a range to become devastated by over-browsing. With more restrictive seasons and harvest limits, an over-hunted deer herd can recover in a few years, but a range destroyed by excessive browsing may not recover for decades.

Above: Biology student at the Adirondack Ecological Center, Huntington Forest, about to radio collar and release a whitetail fawn. The Center is a division of the State University of New York.
Facing page: Whitetail deer bucks. The deep snows of the Adirondacks limit the availability of feed for deer, forcing the animals to "yard up" for the winter in very restricted areas.
PETER LEMON PHOTOS 43

Preferred deer foods include hardwoods like maple, apple, sumac, birch, aspen and cherry, and softwoods like eastern hemlock and white cedar. The most critical time of year for deer is winter, when snow restricts movement and preferred foods may be quickly exhausted. Deer then turn to foods of lower quality and may even die with full stomachs. Deer resorting to low-value foods such as balsam fir, tamarack, spruce or beech weaken and become more vulnerable to disease, predation or harsh weather.

As a result of deer's food preferences, certain plant species are disappearing from the Adirondacks wherever excessive numbers of deer are found. For example, white cedars, particularly young ones, are noticeably missing from many swamps and marshes due to excessive deer browsing. Other species like American beech have increased because deer eat them only as a last resort. Thus, deer browsing is actually changing the composition of the Adirondack forest.

In spite of the early reputation as fine hunting country, the Adirondack Mountains are not productive deer range. Located at the northern edge of whitetail deer distributional range, with heavy snowfall and harsh winters, the Adirondacks are marginal deer habitat compared to areas farther south and at lower elevations. This is reflected in the total deer harvest. In 1986, more than 10,000 deer were taken in Sullivan County in southern New York, while 592 deer were harvested in Warren County in the heart of the Adirondacks.

The Adirondacks' deep snows often force deer into "yards" where they are trapped throughout of the winter. Most deer yards are located among evergreens, such as hemlock or cedar forests along lowland watercourses, which offer shelter from wind and snow and access to preferred browse species.

Moose

Although the Adirondacks are near the northern limits of the whitetail deer distribution, these mountains formed the natural *southern* limit for another member of the deer family—the moose. With their long legs and heavy coats, moose are better adapted for survival in the Adirondacks, particularly at higher elevations. Before Europeans came into the area, moose were far more abundant than deer, but uncontrolled hunting eliminated these animals here by 1861, when the last documented legal kill occurred at Raquette Lake. Eight years later, the New York legislature closed the moose season.

In recent years, moose, thought to be overflow from recovering populations in Vermont, have been invading the Adirondacks. They have been sighted at Cranberry Lake, Loon Lake, Indian Lake and St. Regis Falls, among other areas. One biologist estimates the present Adirondack population at 30 animals, but he cautioned that it could be double that figure, since no one tracks moose numbers in the region.

Most of the moose sighted are male, which is not unusual because, in most mammal species, it is the male that tends to colonize new regions. During the rut, male moose wander widely looking for a mate. One love-smitten, radio-collared Adirondack bull moose traveled west all the way to the Montezuma Wildlife Refuge near Rochester searching unsuccessfully for a female before turning around and coming back to winter in the mountains.

Besides lack of mates, the greatest single limiting factor on moose recolonization appears to be poaching. Illegal killing of these large, relatively slow-moving animals is easy and very few moose survive more than a few years before being shot. The only positive note in this scenario is that moose populations in Vermont slowly are increasing and it's likely that more cow moose will wander into the Adirondack region. With a bit of protection from poaching, moose may once again fill their historic role in the Adirondack fauna.

Black bear

Black bears, although hunted to low numbers, never were fully extirpated from the Adirondacks. With protection, these mountains currently support an estimated population of 3,600 bears. They comprise 90 percent of New York state's bear population. The bear is primarily a vegetarian, although it will eat meat when meat is readily available. Since finding sufficient plant material to keep a bear alive through an Adirondack winter would be impossible, bears evolved the ecological strategy of avoiding food shortages by hibernation.

Hibernation is a behavioral and physiological adaptation that helps conserve energy by reducing metabolic requirements. In the fall, due to decreasing day length, perhaps coupled with the onset of winter weather, the bear seeks out a denning location. In years of food scarcity, bears den earlier than in years of abundance. Females tend to den earlier than the males, who may wander until late November or even December. Conversely, males are the first to emerge in spring.

Den sites are typically in remote, higher-elevation locations amidst heavy forest. Usually a rock cave is the den site, although hollow logs will do. Undoubtedly, in the years

It is doubtful that bears ever will be threatened with total extinction as long as sufficient habitat is maintained and reasonable hunting restrictions are observed.

before logging when larger trees were common, more bears denned inside tree trunks. Cooler and shaded north or east slopes are favored, so that snow is likely to accumulate over the den entrance and insulate it.

Bears do not truly hibernate, which is a state of extremely reduced metabolism from which an animal cannot easily be aroused. Perhaps deep sleep is a better term for the

bear. This may be an adaptation that allows the female to care for the cubs, which are born in mid-winter while the bears are still in their dens.

Female black bears usually don't reach sexual maturity until they are five to seven years old. Since cubs remain with their mother for two years, breeding occurs every other year; hence, the reproductive capacity of the black bear is low. In

Ninety percent of the black bears found in New York State reside in the Adirondacks. The bear has a low biological potential compared to deer and other smaller animals, and thus are much more prone to over-hunting. JOHN SERRAO

Wolves once were found throughout the eastern United States, but were exterminated by early sttlers. Their diet consists of deer and moose, particularly in the winter, while beaver is one of their major food species in the summer. JOHN SERRAO

One can hope that in the not-too-distant future, the howl of the wolf will be heard echoing across the frozen lakes of the region.

spite of this low biological potential, some 747 bears were shot by New York hunters during the 1986 hunting season, with 658 taken from the Adirondacks. Hunting could contribute to a decline in bear numbers. Nevertheless, given the wide distribution of black bears, including in remote wilderness areas, it is doubtful that bears ever will be threatened with total extinction as long as sufficient habitat is maintained and reasonable hunting restrictions are observed.

Wolf

The Adirondack wolf has not been as fortunate as the bear; it was eliminated by the turn of the century. One of the first laws initiated on the frontier established bounties on predators, including the wolf and mountain lion and, in some cases, it even extended to non-predators. Lewis County, for instance, had a two-cent bounty on chipmunks! In the early 1800s, a bountied wolf brought in $60—no small sum in the frontier economy.

One apparent concentration of wolves was in Franklin County, where residents applied for $5,500 in bounty money between 1820 and 1822. Legislators in Albany became suspicious of Franklin County's thriving wolf packs, and the investigators discovered that county residents were bringing in wolf carcasses, applying for the bounty, then leaving with the wolf, which was given to a friend, who would claim a bounty. To thwart illegal claimants, the legislators enacted a thousand-dollar annual ceiling on bounty payments statewide. This legislation apparently brought about an abrupt decline in the Adirondack wolf population, since the number of animals submitted for bounty dropped precipitously.

Although the wolf is gone now, many believe the Adirondack region never will be really wild until wolves once again roam these mountains, and some discuss reintroducing the wolf. There is no biological reason why this should not be successful, but political opposition, particularly from hunters, may be intense. Nevertheless, one can hope that in the not-too-distant future, the howl of the wolf will be heard echoing across the frozen lakes of the region.

If reintroduced, what would wolves eat? Although not fussy about their diets, wolves are primarily predators of big game. In eastern North America, deer and moose are the primary prey species, but wolves also eat mice, rabbits and, in summer, beaver. Although it is almost impossible for wolves to eliminate their prey populations, it is wrong to assume that wolves will have no impact on prey. Wolves may occasionally depress local deer or moose numbers, especially when these are vulnerable during a harsh winter.

In the Adirondack region, wolf predation, particularly when deer are yarded during winter, would benefit plant communities like white cedar and eastern hemlock, both of which suffer from excessive deer browsing. In the end, these plant communities would regain their health and, as a result, their ability to sustain even greater deer populations, which in turn could support more wolves.

The big cats

The wolf is only one missing link in the Adirondack fauna. Another is the mountain lion, also known as puma, catamount or cougar. Between 1871 and 1894, 99 mountain lions were turned in for New York state's $20 bounty. In 1886, Dr. H. Hart Merriam estimated that 100 mountain lions had been killed in the Adirondack Mountains alone since 1860. The last reported Adirondack mountain lion was supposedly killed by Elk Lake in 1908. No live ones have been documented since that time, even though reports of sightings still occur. It is doubtful that any breeding population remains, although the occasional sighting may represent tame lions that have been released by their owners.

Mountain lions, unlike wolves, which run down prey, capture by careful stalking and a pounce, much as our domestic tabby attacks a bird in the yard. Mountain lions prey almost entirely on large ungulates like deer, although they can and do take the porcupine, quills and all—apparently with no ill effect to the lion.

If not persecuted, the secretive mountain lion can survive even in close proximity to humans. Considering the low human population and the abundant habitat found in the Adirondacks, mountain lion reintroduction should succeed if the animals are protected from poaching.

Another cat that was extirpated from the Adirondacks is the lynx, which usually is associated with the deep-snow areas of the boreal forest. Its large feet act like snowshoes, enabling the lynx to travel over deep, soft snow with a minimum of effort. More than most animals, the lynx is tied to its major prey species, the snowshoe hare. These hare populations follow a more or less predictable population build-up followed by a crash that occurs approximately every 10 years. With the loss of its major prey, lynx populations also crash.

The bobcat, a southern cousin of the lynx that has expanded its range into the Adirondack region, inhabits low-elevation areas, particularly near watercourses. Unlike the lynx, the bobcat preys on a variety of animals, including birds, small mammals and even deer. Since the Adirondacks represent the northern range limits for this feline species, it is under unusual stress. There is evidence to suggest that unless the Adirondack bobcat can capture a deer or find a roadkill, they usually won't survive the winter. One study showed that deer comprise 72 percent of a bobcat's winter diet, while hares represented the only other major component, making up 20 percent.

Its large feet act like snowshoes, enabling the lynx to travel over deep, soft snow with a minimum of effort.

Bobcats, pictured here, have expanded their range into the lower elevations of the Adirondacks. Lynxes and mountain lions, once both found here, now are locally extinct, but there are plans to reintroduce the lynx.
PETER LEMON

47

Above: Young short-tailed weasel. One of the most aggressive hunters, the weasel is known to attack animals larger than itself, such as the cottontail rabbit. GERARD LEMMO
Facing page, left: Beavers, once trapped to extinction here, now are quite common in the park. They form colonies and gradually work upstream, constructing new dams along the way. Right: Beaver ponds are essential to the Adirondack web of life. Providing miniature dams that hold run-off, beavers are important in the hydrological cycle. Their ponds create habitat for ducks and other animals and, once filled with silt, become new meadows. GEORGE WUERTHNER PHOTOS

Weasel family

The many members of the weasel family have fared better than cats. The only one not now found in the Adirondacks is the wolverine. Never abundant, this species was last recorded at Raquette River in 1884. The fisher looks like a dark black cat and is one of the larger members of the weasel family. Drastically reduced as a result of habitat changes caused by logging, turn-of-the-century fires and intense trapping pressure (particularly during the 1920s), the fisher was almost extirpated from the region. In 1936, the state finally closed the fisher trapping season and the small remnant populations began to rebuild. Trapping was reopened in 1949, and in the 1985-86 season some 1,524 fishers were taken by state residents.

No one knows how the fisher got its name, but it certainly doesn't have anything to do with its habits or prey. This animal spends most of its time in the hemlock, spruce and fir forests feeding on rabbits, squirrels and porcupine. It is particularly adept at capturing the spiky rodent, and seldom suffers from such encounters.

The pine marten, a smaller member of the weasel family, has not recovered as well as the fisher. The marten, like the fisher, nearly was eliminated from the Adirondacks due to habitat loss resulting from logging combined with uncontrolled trapping pressure. During the 1920s, a marten pelt brought $200—a sizeable amount in those days. Today the average price is less than $20. The state now allows limited trapping and, although the marten still is not common over much of its former range, some 120 marten were trapped in the 1985-86 season.

The pine marten's main haunts are the high elevation spruce-fir forests and it is traditionally common in the High Peaks area, where it preys upon red squirrel, grouse, chipmunks, voles, snowshoe hares and mice. In summer this diet is supplemented with berries and other plants. In addition to the marten, other weasel-family members found in the Adirondacks include the river otter, mink, skunk and weasel.

Beaver

Although nearly all of the weasel family are trapped for their pelts, it is the largest member of the rodent family, the beaver, that generated the trapping era in North America. So complete were the efforts of trappers, that beaver were nearly eliminated from New York state. In 1902, a few pairs were released in remote sections of the Adirondacks and subsequently the beaver prospered. Today it is nearly impossible to take a walk in the Adirondacks without encountering a beaver pond or a trail flooded by beaver dams. In 1985-86, 14,958 beavers were trapped in New York State.

Beavers are, in many ways, one of the most important animals within the Adirondack mountain region. Their dams and resulting small ponds create a giant network of reservoirs, holding back floods and allowing water to slowly saturate the ground. The cumulative influence of countless small dams on water storage is significant.

The ponds themselves serve many other wildlife species, from ducks to brook trout. Songbirds and other animals find ideal habitat at the edges of these ponds. Eventually such waters fill with silt, reverting to meadows and providing one of the major openings in the otherwise dense forest canopy. Beavers are among the prime agents of meadow formation in the Adirondacks.

Other rodent families

A host of smaller mammals—from rabbits and squirrels to mice and voles—make up the bulk of wildlife numbers found in the Adirondack region. Most are nocturnal and small enough to escape notice, but without them many of the larger mammals—in particular predators—would not survive.

The smallest of these mammals are the shrews. There are six species found here, ranging in size from the pygmy shrew (barely 2.5 inches long) to the short-tailed shrew, at 4.5 inches, the largest species.

Because of their large surface to volume ratio, shrews must eat almost constantly to stay alive, and can die within 24 hours if deprived of food. They often eat twice their weight a day, never resting more than a few hours between feeding bouts.

Perhaps the most unusual shrew is the northern water shrew, which dives underwater to capture larvae of aquatic insects. When it dives, its fur traps air, encasing the animal in a watertight suit.

Shrews often are confused with moles, another member of the *Insectivora* order. Both live underground burrowing

through the soil and leaf litter looking for insects. Moles rely entirely upon tactile senses to locate food, because they are almost blind.

At night, one is apt to find mice, voles and jumping mice scampering about the woods. Perhaps the most interesting of this group are the two species of jumping mouse: the woodland jumping mouse and meadow jumping mouse. Both have large hind legs and long tails similar to the kangaroo rats found in the West and both bounce around woodlands at night foraging on seeds and grains. Unlike mice and voles, these two jumping mouse species store up thick layers of fat during the summer and fall, and then hibernate through the winter in underground burrows.

Voles look like tiny mice with short tails and rounded ears. The most common species in the Adirondacks is the redback vole which, as its name implies, has a bright rust-colored back. It is common in the spruce-fir forests where it makes its home. The rarest Adirondack vole is the yellownose vole which inhabits only the highest rocky summits. These creatures probably are the highest-elevation year-round New York residents—I once saw one of these critters right at the top of Mount Marcy!

Looking very much like a vole with tiny ears and a short tail is the northern bog lemming. It is found in bogs and dense meadows in the northeast Adirondacks, where it reaches its southern range limits. Very little is known about this rare Adirondack mammal.

Above the normal forest-floor habitat of the voles, up in the trees, one might catch glimpses of one of the most usual Adirondack mammals, the flying squirrel. There are two species of these nocturnal forest dwellers: the eastern flying squirrel and the northern flying squirrel. Both acquired their name because of their gliding descents from tree to tree. This is accomplished by a loose fold of skin that extends from the front leg to the hind leg and becomes taut like a sail when the squirrel stretches its limbs.

Both squirrels are cavity nesters that inhabit abandoned woodpecker holes within old snags. Extensive fires and logging that eliminated much of the old-growth Adirondack forests must have had a disastrous impact on populations of these animals. In the winter as many as 20 squirrels jam into the same cavity to conserve heat, but they live alone throughout the remainder of the year.

Birdlife

Except for a few of the larger mammals, most visitors to the Adirondacks will see birds more than anything else. The first person to catalog Adirondack birds was Theodore Roosevelt, who spent three boyhood summers at Paul Smith's resort near St. Regis Lake. Roosevelt listed 97 species, of the more than 225 species known for the Adirondack region today. Several birds are especially interesting.

It may be surprising to learn that both golden and bald eagles occasionally are seen here. The golden is much more common in the western United States, but is known to nest on cliffs in the Adirondacks. It hunts mammals, primarily on open slopes. As hill farms were abandoned and forest clearings grew over, this bird gradually disappeared, with the last verified reproduction occurring in 1970. The bald eagle, primarily a fish eater, once was fairly common in the Adirondack region, but the use of chlorinated hydrocarbons like DDT resulted in weakened egg structure and a subsequent decline in this species. At present there are three known nesting pairs of bald eagles in New York State, none in the Adirondacks.

Like the eagle, the peregrine falcon was another Adirondack resident that suffered from thin eggshells as a result of DDT. It never had been numerous, with no more than 12 or so nesting pairs in the Adirondacks in pre-DDT days. The last successful Adirondack peregrine nesting took place in 1961. Since the early 1970s, captive falcons at Cornell University have been producing young that have been reintroduced into former habitats, like the Adirondacks, in an effort to recover peregrine populations. During 1986, 21 peregrine falcons were placed in the wild, including several Adirondack locations, as part of New York's restoration effort.

An avian predator slowly making a comeback without the aid of humans is the raven, the largest member of the

Left: *Great crested flycatcher.*
Above: *Male wood duck with mallards. Wood ducks typically nest in cavities of dead trees near water, such as those often found in beaver ponds.*
GERARD LEMMO PHOTOS

Like the eagle, the peregrine falcon was an Adirondack resident that suffered from thin eggshells as a result of DDT.

One of the most cherished of Adirondack birds is the common loon.

dependent upon carrion for part of their food. Predators like wolves and mountain lions provided ravens with a source of winter food because they sometimes left behind part of their kill. Once these predators were eliminated, survival became more difficult for ravens and they disappeared. Today, winter raven food is provided by human garbage and road-kills, which have increased substantially especially with increased winter road traffic associated with travel to ski resorts.

One of the most cherished of Adirondack birds is the common loon. Known for its plaintive wail and its striking black and white plumage, the loon has been declining throughout its natural range. Research has shown that loons typically inhabit larger lakes, usually more than 25 acres in size. This in itself is a somewhat limiting factor here, since there are only 450 lakes of that size or larger in the Adirondack Park. In a recent survey conducted in northern New York, only 128 lakes had any evidence of breeding loons, and breeding pairs totaled 157. The adult loon population within this study area is estimated to be 561.

Loons are highly sensitive to disturbance while on the nest and some biologists speculate that one reason for the decline in loon numbers may be the increase in human recreation on many Adirondack lakes. Acid rain also may be making an impact. The loon is a fish-eater, and acidification is affecting reproduction and growth of many Adirondack fish populations, although at present mostly in the smaller water bodies that loons seldom utilize.

Other rare or unusual bird species known to frequent the Adirondacks include: ring-necked ducks, goldeneyes, Lincoln's sparrows, red crossbills, Canada jays, goshawks, spruce grouse, gray-cheeked thrushes and brown-capped chickadees.

Salmon

One of the wildlife success stories of the Adirondacks is the return of the salmon. When Samuel Champlain first explored the lake that now bears his name, landlocked salmon spawned in swarms in many of the rivers draining into the lake. So numerous were the salmon during their spawning runs that one early settler recounted how crossing rivers on horseback was hazardous because there were so many salmon that they "would run against the [horse's] legs with great force and impetuosity," often startling the animals. Early settlers exploited this natural bounty, even harvesting fish by the wagonload, with pitchforks.

crow family. This highly intelligent and adaptable bird is found throughout North America, from the deserts of the southwest to the arctic tundra in Alaska east to the Adirondacks, yet for some unexplained reason it began to disappear from New York by the early 1900s. Then, in 1968, a few ravens were sighted around Giant Mountain and at least one pair nested. Gradually the population built up so that it is at least not unusual to spot a raven while climbing in the High Peaks and elsewhere. Ravens nest early in the season, mating as early as March. They tend to nest on cliff faces, and so places like Chapel Pond and the Cascades Lakes are good locations to spot nesting ravens.

Although no one knows exactly why ravens might have disappeared, one speculation is that in winter they are

Although excessive exploitation probably contributed to the salmon's demise, dams also had their impact. Dams built to provide waterpower for mills could be found on nearly all the major rivers entering Lake Champlain. Coupled with the barriers created by dams, logging and agricultural practices contributed to increased siltation and higher river-water temperatures, which killed young salmon fry.

Efforts at salmon-run restoration were begun in the 1950s, but not until 1973 was a major salmon restocking program initiated. Young salmon are stocked in parent streams where they grow to about six inches in length. At this stage, when they are called smolts, they migrate downriver to a large body of water—in this case, Lake Champlain—where they remain for about two years. Feeding upon a rich diet of smelt, the salmon grow rapidly and reach lengths of 20 to 25 inches and weights up to five pounds. Unlike Pacific salmon species that die after spawning, landlocked Atlantic salmon may spawn several times. The Saranac and Boquet Rivers are among the Lake Champlain streams once again experiencing salmon runs. Landlocked salmon also are found in Thirteenth Lake and Lake George, among others.

MANAGEMENT

It is becoming increasingly clear to many biologists that if we wish to maintain biological diversity and representative species and their habitats, we must begin to think in terms of ecosystem management. This includes protection of all representative habitats, travel corridors and biological influences, which may include wild fire, insect outbreaks and other naturally occurring events. The Adirondack Park represents the best opportunity for a wilderness recovery program to be found on the entire East Coast, but there are some critical shortcomings to correct, including acquisition of a significant representation of the spruce boreal forest in the northeast portion of the park. In addition, all extirpated wildlife species must be considered potential candidates for reintroduction efforts, including the wolf and the mountain lion. Only when these goals are accomplished will it be proper to say that the Adirondacks are truly "forever wild."

Blue jay. GERARD LEMMO

HISTORY

4

The Lake Champlain corridor was an early hotbed of military action. Cannons at Fort Ticonderoga are shown here. The fort was built by the French and known as Fort Carillon, but the British overran it in 1759 and renamed it Ticonderoga. The capture of Ticonderoga by Ethan Allen and his Green Mountain Boys in 1775 signaled the start of the American Revolution
GEORGE WUERTHNER

The Adirondacks always have been an island of wildness. The rugged terrain and harsh climate have discouraged settlement by humans and even many wildlife species. Consider that much of the western United States had been explored and mapped before anyone had even surveyed the High Peaks region in the 1830s. Mt. Marcy, only 5,344', was not climbed until 1837, just a few years before John Fremont was scaling 13,000' peaks in Wyoming's Wind River Range.

Although white settlement gradually invaded the lower elevation areas, few settlers actually penetrated the mountains. The climate and poor soils did as much as anything to discourage them. Winter snowfalls average from 90" to 165" annually (depending upon the range and the elevation) and temperatures are low. The town of Stillwater along the western edge claims the dubious distinction of having recorded New York's coldest temperature of 52° below zero. The growing season usually is shorter than 100 days, and the mountainous terrain, coupled with the abundance of swamps and marshes that cover some 15 percent of the lowland areas, leave little land suitable for agriculture.

TOUGH EXISTENCE

Those animals and individuals that do reside here often live a marginal existence. There are some individuals—human and otherwise—who could not survive elsewhere; the Adirondack terrain is best suited to their habitat requirements. But for most, whether whitetail deer that wander the High Peaks or people who remain year-round in places like Lake Placid, Old Forge or Tupper Lake, better climate and opportunities for making a living can be found outside of these mountains.

In the days before the European invasion of North America, no humans lived in these mountains year-round. The Algonquin Indians lived to the north along the St. Lawrence, and to the west and southwest were the Iroquois. It was easier then, as now, to live in the lowlands. Game and fish, though seemingly plentiful in the Adirondacks of today, could be had in greater abundance in the then-undeveloped lowlands. In addition, farming—one of the main sources of food for all Northeast Indian tribes—was possible only in the warmer lower-elevation areas. Indians, no doubt, passed through the Adirondacks, especially along the eastern edge in the Champlain Valley, but few lingered long in these forested highlands.

CONFLICT

The Lake Champlain-Lake George corridor linking the St. Lawrence and Hudson River watersheds was a major Indian travel route. It was here that, in 1609, the Frenchman Samuel Champlain, along with a group of Algonquins from the St. Lawrence region, battled a group of Iroquois. Some historians credit this encounter with changing the course of North American history. Champlain killed two Iroquois with a shot from his harquebus, and the Iroquois, never on cordial relations with their Algonquin northern neighbors, added the French to their list of enemies. When hostilities later broke out between the French and British over domination of the New World, the Iroquois sided with the English, eventually forcing the French to give up claims to North America.

The Adirondacks became a battleground between these two opposing Indian groups and their European allies. The French and the Dutch, and later the English, set up trading posts on the fringes of the region and began to offer European goods in exchange for furs—in particular that of beaver, which was in high demand in Europe for the manufacture of hats. Albany was originally a Dutch settlement known as Beverwyck, then New Orange. It became Albany after the British assumed control of all the Dutch North American holdings in 1664. Although the town eventually would become the capital of New York state, it had its beginnings as

The climate and poor soils of the mountains did much to discourage early settlers.

"Surrender of Fort William Henry, August 1757, Lake George, New York." Painting by J.L.G. Ferris (1863-1930). COURTESY OF THE GLENS FALLS INSURANCE COMPANY, A MEMBER OF THE CONTINENTAL INSURANCE COMPANIES

thousand French settlers and soldiers were living along Champlain's shores at strategic locations such as Crown Point and the Alburg Peninsula. The British attempted to protect the northern flank of their colonies by building Fort William Henry in 1755 at the south end of Lake George. In the same year, the French built Fort Carillon 30 miles to the north at a narrows in Lake Champlain. Tensions between the rival empires finally erupted in 1757 when the French successfully overran Fort William Henry, although the British recaptured it. Then in 1759, under Geoffrey Amherst, they managed to storm Carillon and put it under British control, renaming it Fort Ticonderoga. The French were routed northward and eventually all the way out of Canada, enabling the British to control most of the eastern coast of North America.

Fewer than 20 years later, in 1775, the British would lose Ticonderoga when Ethan Allen and his Green Mountain Boys, along with Benedict Arnold and some Massachusetts regulars, captured the fort in what became one of the opening battles of the American Revolution. As in the French and Indian Wars, the Champlain Valley became a crucial military theater as Americans and British vied for control. But that is getting ahead of the story.

Following the British takeover of the Champlain valley in 1759, a few colonial families ventured north to settle the rich Champlain valley. One of the first settlements was Willsboro, founded by William Gilliland in 1765 near the mouth of the Boquet River. The colony prospered and Gilliland became lord of a small wilderness empire. But his fortune turned during the American revolution. Gilliland was accused of being a traitor by none other than Benedict Arnold, and subsequently was jailed. Later, he lost his land and property and ended in debtor's prison. He died of exposure on a cold winter night in 1796, and the only reminder of this once wealthy man are the names of the villages he helped found—Willsboro and Elizabethtown, named for his wife.

Although a few intrepid settlers like Gilliland continued to eye the Champlain region, uncertainty over the legal status of Adirondack lands, as well as the lake corridor's use as a major military pathway, discouraged further settlement until the formation of a new government after the Revolution would resolve these issues.

a fur trading post. Some 35,000 beaver and otter pelts had been shipped from here by 1656. To the north, Montreal was the focus of the fur trade in French-claimed territories.

The demand for furs lured Indians into the beaver-rich Adirondacks, and competition between Iroquois and Algonquin developed over these trapping grounds, especially after they had depleted areas closer to home. The fur trade heightened the existing antagonism between the Indians, and eventually the two Indian groups were drawn into the conflict between the French and British. This struggle raged for more than a hundred years in North America—much of it in the Lake Champlain–Lake George corridor—under the collective title of the French and Indian Wars.

The French were the first to set up a base of operations. In 1666, they constructed Ft. St. Anne on Isle La Motte at the north end of Lake Champlain. By the 1730s, more than a

SPECULATION

Despite a lack of settler interest in these uplands, land speculation attracted its share of wheeler-dealers. In 1771, two shipwrights, Joseph Totten and Stephen Crossfield, acting as front men for the Jessup Brothers, businessmen in Albany, petitioned the governor of New York to purchase 800,000 acres (it was later discovered the purchase contained 1,150,000 acres) from the Mohawk Indians in the southern Adirondacks. The tract included such well known Adirondack features as Indian and Raquette lakes. The Jessups hoped to divide this land into tracts to sell to other developers. Unfortunately for the brothers, the American Revolution nullified the purchase and the tract reverted to the newly-formed state of New York.

The state, finding itself capital-poor, but land-rich, decided to sell as much of its undeveloped real estate as possible. In 1784, New York passed a law to speed the sale of "waste and unappropriated lands within the State." Despite the fact that few investors actually saw the land they bought, interest in land speculation remained high. One such investor, Alexander Macomb, bought 3.63 million acres of this "wasteland" in 1792 for 16¢ an acre. This tract—the largest single land sale in New York State history and known thereafter as Macomb's Tract—included what today are parts of Franklin, St. Lawrence, Herkimer, Hamilton, Lewis, Jefferson and Oswego counties.

Above: *Graveyard at Port Henry on Lake Champlain. The Lake Champlain region was the first area to be settled by whites. Port Henry was one of the early iron mining centers.*
Above left: *John Brown started a farm near North Elba where he taught northern agricultural techniques to slaves smuggled out of the South on the Underground Railroad.*
Left: *Ruins at Crown Point on Lake Champlain. First settled by the French, Crown Point later passed into British hands.*
GEORGE WUERTHNER PHOTOS

A view of the reconstructed interior of a typical "camp" at the Blue Mountain Museum. PETER LEMMON

In the early 1800s, the rocky and thin soils, coupled with the lack of navigable rivers, made the region seem inhospitable to human settlement.

In the early 1800s, the rocky and thin soils, coupled with the lack of navigable rivers, made the region seem inhospitable to human settlement. The rocks did harbor some mineral wealth and this soon caught the eye of developers. As early as the 1700s, Adirondack promoters including William Gilliland had found iron ore near Lake Champlain. Americans at Fort Ticonderoga may have worked some deposits near Port Henry. Many of the early villages in or around the Adirondack region had their own iron forges, and each required charcoal—600 bushels to produce one ton of metal from every four tons of ore. Logging for charcoal production was one of the first uses of the vast Adirondack forests. In many areas, the availability of trees for charcoal limited the iron output. Besides, many Adirondack ore deposits had impurities that made iron production difficult.

One of the most famous Adirondack ironworks was developed at Tahawus. In 1826, Archibald McIntyre and his son-in-law David Henderson investigated a deposit near Lake Placid, brought to their attention by an Indian who said he knew the location of a large iron ore bed. (The names of Mt. McIntyre and Henderson Lake commemorate these two early Adirondackers.) Following their guide through what is now Indian Pass, to the headwaters of the Hudson River below Mt. Marcy, McIntyre and Henderson found pieces of nearly pure iron lying in the river channel.

The men quickly bought title to the surrounding lands and, by 1839, had developed the site into a small town that included a bank, school and housing for nearly 200 workers—all located in the midst of nearly untrod wilderness. But the mine operations were troubled by "impurities" in the ore, which made it difficult to process. On top of that, the distance to markets over rough and uncertain roads further eroded the profitability of the operation. Eventually the mine closed. When it was reopened in the 20th century, it was found that the impurity that so hampered the early iron masters was titanium—useful as a white pigment in paint and as a heat-resistant metal for engines.

Other early mining operations were developed at Lyon Mountain and Mineville near Port Henry. At one time or another more than two hundred Adirondack iron ore deposits were worked. But better grade iron ore was discovered in the Midwest and easier shipment via the Great Lakes eventually doomed all but the most profitable Adirondack operations.

Macomb eventually went bankrupt and his lands were split among his backers. Some found themselves with acreage near Plattsburgh, or along the St. Lawrence River, and settlement rapidly followed. But no one penetrated the heart of the mountains. Even though roads like the Malone-to-Plattsburgh trail were built before 1800, these skirted the mountains and the interior remained an unknown wilderness.

Besides private purchases, the state set aside a 665,000-acre tract in the Adirondacks, where Revolutionary War veterans were entitled to select parcels as payment for military services. But the state had put aside other tracts in western New York, which contained better land, and no claim was made in the Adirondacks. The Old Military Tract, as it was called, eventually was subdivided into 12 parcels and sold to speculators, but no one could be persuaded to settle on them.

Most of what would later become the Adirondack Park was within these three large tracts, which the state managed to dispose of—with great difficulty—by 1800. Later, New York State would have to work even harder to buy back this watery, mosquito-ridden wasteland, of course at much greater expense.

Other minerals mined from the Adirondacks include talc and zinc. More zinc is found at the Balmat mine than anywhere else in the country. Garnet, mined near Gore Mountain, is used in sandpaper and emery boards and for other abrasive materials. Finally, there is graphite—the "lead" used in the familiar yellow Ticonderoga pencils—mined along Lake Champlain. But mining tends to be cyclic and today except for the Gore Mountain garnets, all other operations are closed.

AGRICULTURE

Mining provided jobs in a few scattered locations, and hence led to organization of towns, but it was farming that stimulated most of the original settlement of the region—at least along the fringes of the mountains. In the late 1700s and early 1800s, settlers moved north to avail themselves of free or cheap land. Most agriculture was centered where it still is found today: along the Lake Champlain lowlands. But the flow of settlers dwindled after 1820, when better farmlands became available in the Ohio Valley and farther west. These early subsistence farmers raised wheat, corn and a few animals, and made potash from ashes of the trees they cleared from the fields. Potash was an important ingredient in the manufacture of explosives and soap. Thirty cords of wood were required to make one sixth of a ton of potash worth $15 to $20.

Much of the frontier agricultural production flowed north to Canada rather than south, because the easiest travel route was along Lake Champlain. Trade was brisk in spite of an embargo upon trade with England and Canada enacted in 1807 by President Thomas Jefferson. Even the formal declaration of war against England at the start of the War of 1812 failed to stem this flow of illegal goods. Many frontiersmen ignored the order, and Sir George Provost, Governor of Canada, boasted that most of the British troops in Canada were eating beef produced in the United States.

But even as American trade goods were flowing north to Canada, British forces were readying themselves for a push southward via the Champlain–Lake George corridor. A British fleet sailed southward in the spring of 1814. Off Valcour Island, they encountered Lt. Thomas Macdonough commanding a hastily constructed American fleet that engaged the vastly superior British forces in what is known as the Battle of Plattsburgh. Although suffering extensive losses, Macdonough managed to rout the enemy. On land, 4,700 troops under General Macomb held back nearly triple their

number in British soldiers, who—after learning of their fleet's defeat—retreated northward to Canada. Thus the Americans were saved from an attack through their back door.

Above: Charcoal kilns near Clintonville. Charcoal was an essential ingredient for the production of iron and much of the early logging of the vast Adirondack forests was done to provide for the charcoal kilns.
Left: Hunting was, and still is, a major attraction of the Adirondack region. Excessive hunting led to the extinction of many species, including moose. Seneca Ray Stoddard photo. IMAGES COURTESY CHAPMAN HISTORICAL MUSEUM, GLENS FALLS

VERPLANCK COLVIN

Twenty-two years before the Adirondack Park was created, Colvin argued for protection of the area's watersheds. Here, swollen by spring rains, is Roaring Brook Falls. K.A. WILSON

No person ever knew the Adirondacks as well as Verplanck Colvin, and probably no one was more passionate in their defense during the years when the first Forest Preserve was established.

Colvin grew up in Albany, where his father was a prominent lawyer. Young Verplanck was expected to follow in his father's footsteps, but at an early age developed passions for the outdoors and for map-making. Although he finished his law studies, Colvin abandoned a law career and began to climb mountains, beginning with the nearby Adirondacks and moving west. After his western adventures, he spent the next 30 years crusading for the preservation of the Adirondacks.

In 1868, just 21 years old, Colvin made his first public plea for the protection of the Adirondacks. He implored a crowd gathered in Lake Pleasant, New York on the southern fringe of the mountains, to work toward the creation of a state park. Comparing the Adirondacks to areas he had recently visited on his western travels, he told the crowd that the Adirondacks were no less beautiful than the Grand Canyon or the Rockies.

Independently wealthy, Colvin spent a good deal of his youth exploring the Adirondack region. In 1870, when he asked the Board of Regents of New York State to perform a major survey to determine state holdings, he used an economic argument (as conservationists even today must do). He wrote that the mountains "contain the springs which are the sources of our principal rivers and feeders of the canals. Each summer the water supply for these rivers and canals is lessened, and commerce has suffered." To ensure the preservation of the watershed, Colvin felt the only solution was to prohibit logging in the Adirondacks.

Although he was an excellent surveyor and map maker, Colvin appears to have had little sympathy for the discomforts encountered by himself or his crew. He was quite content to survive on stale bread and half-cooked trout. He never expected more of his crews than he himself was willing to do, but his commitment and enthusiasm far surpassed those of anyone he was able to hire. His description of one incident bears this out. "Here the guides, dissatisfied with the severity of the labor, demanded their discharge and asked increased pay: nor could they be persuaded to proceed further, exhibiting their torn clothing and soleless gaping boots as evidence of their inability."

So driven was Colvin that he often worked throughout the winter, despite the cold. He reported "The wild winter gale swept over the rocky isle with such violence as to almost extinguish our fire. A fearful night which none of the party will be able to forget. The men fought the cold

by stamping and chopping by turns, snatching some sleep occasionally when the fire could be maintained."

In his years of exploration he was first to climb many of the higher peaks and during September of 1872 he made his most famous discovery during an ascent of Mount Marcy. As he described it "dripping with the moisture of the heavens, it seemed in its minuteness and its prettiness, a veritable Tear-of-the-Clouds, the summit water as I named it." So it remains, Lake Tear of the Clouds, highest source of the Hudson River.

Colvin lived to see the Adirondacks protected with the creation of the Forest Preserve in 1885 and the Adirondack Park in 1892, but something happened to him in his later years. In 1900, he quit his job and seemed to withdraw to himself. Wandering the streets of Albany alone, he often was heard talking to himself. People thought he was insane. He died friendless in a mental hospital in 1920.

But Verplanck Colvin is not forgotten in the mountains he loved. Mount Colvin in the High Peaks is named for the man who probably did more than anyone else to establish the Adirondack Park.

Above: Clifford Brooks Falls near Keene. Colvin was captivated by the beauty of the Adirondacks and he worked harder than anyone else to see that the area was made into a park. GEORGE WUERTHNER ***Above left:*** *Lake Tear of the Clouds, source of the Hudson, was named by Verplanck Colvin.* SENECA RAY STODDARD PHOTO COURTESY OF CHAPMAN HISTORICAL MUSEUM, GLENS FALLS

WOOD INDUSTRY

The conclusion of the War of 1812 gave the United States control of lands in the Midwest, and American settlers began to move into the Ohio Valley. Interest in homesteading Adirondack farmlands dwindled. The rocky uplands would not make good farmland, but the resource they had in abundance was trees, and this did not go unnoticed. As early as 1806, the New York State Legislature passed a law making the Salmon River in Franklin County a public highway, so that logs could be driven down without interference from shoreline-property owners. Later, other rivers were added to the list of "public highways" and the Adirondack logging boom was on. Glens Falls, Albany and, later, Tupper Lake all had their share of mills. The wood industry was for many years the number-one activity in the region.

At first the massive white pine was the preferred species, and loggers selectively cut only these trees. After the development of the sulfite paper process in the 1860s, timbermen began to harvest spruce and fir. Eventually, a rail network enabled even hardwoods to become pulpwood, and clear-cuts became the favored timber harvest method. (Previously, hardwoods had been ignored because they would not float and thus could not be driven on rivers to the mills.) The lumber companies bought up thousands of acres of Adirondack timberlands, cut it over, then abandoned it to the state in lieu of taxes. By 1885, it was estimated that at least two thirds of the Adirondack forest had been cut over.

TOURISM

About this time some prominent New York citizens began to express concern that, if left unchecked, loggers would soon denude the entire region and leave it as a barren wasteland. This change in attitude coincided with a demographic change in our nation. By the late 1800s, much of the country already was settled, and San Francisco, New York, Chicago and Washington, D.C. were well on their way to status as world-class cities. The percentage of the population residing on farms or in rural areas was decreasing and our nation was becoming a country of city dwellers. These urban residents began to long for the rigors, adventure and perceived simplicity of the frontier past. For many, these still could be found in the Adirondacks. People were drawn to the Adirondacks not to take away its timber or mine its ore, but to soak in its beauty and wildness. They would spawn a new Adirondack industry, the one that dominates the region today: tourism.

The first record of what could be called a tourist excursion dates from 1818, when a group of Yale College men visited the southwest Adirondacks merely to fish and rest amid the forested hills. By the 1820s, resorts catering to the American and European upper class were becoming fashionable, with Saratoga Springs just south of the Adirondacks one of the most famous. A few Saratoga visitors and other city dwellers began to explore the wildlands to the north, where rumor told of unrivaled good fishing and hunting.

MAPPING & EXPLORATION

This provoked interest in New York's natural assets and in 1836 the New York Legislature appropriated $100,000 for a

natural-history survey. Exploration of the northern wilderness was assigned to Dr. Ebenezer Emmons, a professor at Williams College in Massachusetts. From a base at the Tahawus mining operations near the headwaters of the Hudson, Emmons proceeded to explore the High Peaks region. He named it the Adirondack, supposedly for a local Indian tribe; the New York Legislature approved the name in 1837. Also in 1837, Emmons climbed the highest peak in this group near the Hudson headwaters and named it Marcy after New York's Governor William L. Marcy, who had supported the Emmons survey.

The view from the top of Mt. Marcy moved Emmons and his party to voice their awe over the still unbroken

Mt. Marcy from Keene Valley in 1888. Tourism was already a major industry in the Adirondack region by this date. SENECA RAY STODDARD PHOTO COURTESY CHAPMAN HISTORICAL MUSEUM, GLENS FALLS

By 1885, it was estimated that at least two thirds of the Adirondack forest had been cut over.

63

He wrote of catching 50 trout in two hours and of other visitors who took fish of up to 19 pounds.

wilderness and its beauty. John Cheney, Emmons' guide, was said to have remarked upon Marcy's summit: "It makes a man feel what it is to have all creation placed beneath his feet." The Emmons party may have been one of the first to describe the Adirondacks' natural attributes not as adversarial, but as worthy of respect and wonder. At this early time, the idea was irregular if not radical.

One of the first descriptive travel pieces to expound upon the Adirondacks' recreational opportunities was written by Joel T. Headley. His book, *The Adirondacks, or Life in the Woods*, helped to popularize the region. He wrote of catching 50 trout in two hours and of other visitors who took fish of up to 19 pounds. To many a citybound reader, such tales were bound to elicit an urge to visit the region, and many did. Besides enjoying themselves in the outdoors, some of these early travelers and writers claimed almost miraculous changes in health and state of mind from their wilderness sojourns, and helped to popularize the idea that breathing the scents of fir and spruce would cure all kinds of ailments.

In the summer of 1858, the Adirondacks were visited by a group of nine men later known as the "Philosophers Club,"

who came to relax in the wilderness. Among them were Louis Agassiz, a Harvard professor and one of the most famous scientists of his day; Ralph Waldo Emerson, poet and transcendentalist; John Holmes, Oliver Wendell's brother; Judge Ebenezer Rockwood Hoar, later U.S. Attorney General; and William James Stillman, journalist and artist. Emerson, perhaps the most eloquent of the group, felt that man was at his best when communicating with nature. To Emerson and many of his colleagues, the Adirondacks were cathedrals where one could get closer to the Creator.

Such a view of mountains could be expected to appeal to those of a religious bent. One of the most ardent and articulate early supporters of the Adirondacks as a spiritual place was the Reverend Mr. William Henry Harrison Murray—later to be known as Adirondack Murray. Mr. Murray was a young and energetic preacher whose sermons always made comparisons between the natural world and heavenly salvation. Murray once wrote "A church under good preaching is like a pond of water when a breeze is on it; it is full of movement and ripple. Timid preaching makes stagnant churches."

Murray was anything but timid in his admiration and enthusiasm for the Adirondacks. After each hunting and fishing trip to the mountains, he would praise the spiritual values to be found in wilderness. He began to publish accounts of his adventures in New England papers. For Murray, like the wilderness spokesman who would follow him, John Muir, nature and God were one, and the best way to get close to God was to visit the mountains.

In 1869, a collection of Murray's newspaper articles were bound in a small book titled *Adventures in the Wilderness or Camp Life in the Adirondacks*. The volume apparently hit a popular chord in the post-Civil War nation, for Murray's book of simple camping adventures was reprinted 10 times in three months, and thousands of people packed up and headed to the Adirondacks seeking both adventure and religious salvation. Advised Murray: "Let the old, old nurse, Nature…take you to her bosom again; and you will return to the city happier and healthier for the embrace."

Many were disappointed in what they found— mosquitoes, cut-over hills, drenching rains and crude accommodations—but for others the Adirondacks were everything promised and more. By 1875, there were more than 200 hotels and inns catering to the growing legions of visitors. In 1871, Thomas Durant, one of the builders of the

Union Pacific Railroad, constructed a line from Saratoga to North Creek, reaching deep into the Adirondack wilderness. Durant's railroad dabbled in the usual lumber and iron, but also transported ever-increasing numbers of tourists.

PRESERVATION

As more and more people penetrated the mountains, there grew a rising concern about the eventual loss of this earthly paradise because of logging. As early as 1857, S.H. Hammond, another Adirondack adventurer and author of *Wild Northern Scenes,* first suggested giving the Adirondack forest some protection. Writing about the forest destruction just then reaching the Raquette Lake country, Hammond asked: "When that time shall have arrived [when logging had destroyed the region] where shall we go to find the woods, the wild things, the old forests? Had I my way I would mark out a circle of a hundred miles in diameter and throw around it the protecting aegis of the constitution. I would make it a forest forever."

COLVIN

While Hammond may have been one of the first to advocate a park in the Adirondacks, Verplanck Colvin, an independently wealthy Albany resident and lawyer by trade, became one of the most ardent supporters of an Adirondack park. Colvin was no stranger to the Adirondacks, having adventured in the wilderness just north of Albany since his teens. He spent his entire adult life working in and exploring the wildlands he had grown to love. And he advocated, more loudly and more consistently than anyone before him, that the region should be protected for future generations as a wilderness park.

While the idea of preserving wilderness for its own sake still is widely debated even today, it was an almost alien notion in the 1870s when America was trying to tame its western landscape and its original inhabitants—the Indians, wolves, grizzlies and bison. But Colvin had other reasons for preservation of the Adirondacks, and it had a decidedly more utilitarian appeal. He argued that the reckless logging of the mountains would destroy the Adirondack watersheds and downstream users of the water would ultimately be the losers. The argument began to make sense to pragmatic New York State businessmen dependent upon the Erie Canal and the Hudson River for transportation and commerce.

A *survey party camped by Long Lake in 1888.* CHAPMAN HISTORICAL MUSEUM

In 1868, Colvin began his campaign to preserve the Adirondacks. Giving speeches, writing articles and letters, he began to enlist support for his proposal. He sent copies of his recommendations for a forest preserve or park to the Board of Regents, who believed the arguments merited the attention of Governor John Hoffman. Hoffman mentioned it in his annual message to the legislature, which already was aware of the destruction of the Adirondacks—from letters written by Colvin and others.

In 1872, the legislature created a Commission of State Parks and appointed a committee, which included Colvin, to study the possibility of creating a park within the Adirondack region. Colvin also was given the job of state surveyor and directed to prepare an accurate and complete map of the region.

The following year Colvin turned in two reports. One described in vivid detail his first year's survey efforts. Writing more in the style of an adventure story than of a stuffy government report, Colvin described the mapping progress, and provided his observations on weather, terrain, adventures and joys encountered along the way. The report was so exciting and filled with such detail about the landscape that people bought it (and copies of seven other survey reports produced during the following years) just for reading pleasure.

Many were disappointed in what they found—mosquitoes, cut-over hills, drenching rains and crude accommodations—but for others the Adirondacks were everything promised and more.

The second report Colvin submitted in 1872 summed up the conclusions of the State Parks Commission. It warned of the expected consequences for the state's water supply if logging in the Adirondacks was not controlled. In many ways, Colvin's conclusions were very similar to those of George Perkins Marsh, who wrote the 1864 book *Man and Nature*—one of the first treatises that discussed ecological relationships. Marsh, a Vermonter, had traveled widely in Europe and the Middle East, and was one of the first people to elucidate the relationship between poor forestry practices and the subsequent erosion, flooding and destruction of watersheds.

By 1880, Colvin had completed his topographical survey of the mountains and had begun to sort out the conflicting boundary lines between privately and publicly owned lands, in dispute since the first Adirondack land sales in the 18th century. New York gradually was acquiring a great deal of Adirondack land abandoned by lumber companies. Many loggers did not even bother to find out who owned the land, and cut at random. To stop this timber piracy, Colvin began redoing the old surveys, and made accurate maps that delineated state as well as private ownership.

CONTROVERSY

The battle to save the Adirondacks was assisted by the beginnings of the national park system. Yellowstone National Park had been created in 1872, the nation's first national park, dedicated not to exploitation of resources but designed to preserve the landscape in its natural state for future generations. It was a powerful idea and other national parks—Yosemite and the Grand Canyon—soon followed. The philosophy behind them lent credibility to New York's own park aspirations.

In 1883, the legislature passed a law forbidding any further sale of state-owned lands in the Adirondacks, thus signaling a change in attitude: The state recognized wildlands as an asset, not an obstacle.

Meanwhile, discussion of the preserve idea was widespread, with many periodicals running editorials both for and against it. The strongest support for some kind of park or preserve was found in New York City. The New York Board of Trade and Transportation stated that "...watersheds are a mighty asset of the Empire State, and it has persistently followed the policy of protecting them as being essential to the commercial, industrial, and transportation interests of the commonwealth." Another supporter was the New York State Chamber of Commerce, which advocated the purchase of 4 million acres of Adirondack land for a preserve. When the idea was debated in the state assembly, one of its most ardent supporters was assemblyman Theodore Roosevelt, who gave a speech about forest destruction and its consequences in France, and how New York faced a similar fate if it refused to do something about protecting the mountains.

In 1884, the legislature appointed a commission headed by Professor Charles Sargent, a proponent of "scientific forestry," which was widely practiced in Europe and was just coming into fashion in the United States. The Sargent Commission was to study the feasibility of establishing a forest preserve system within the state. The commission held hearings all summer and issued its report early in 1885. Among other things, it indicted the timber barons as thieves who were reducing "this region to an unproductive and dangerous desert."

Despite much spirited opposition, the legislature created the Forest Preserve in 1885. Section 8 of the act said: "The lands now or here after constituting the Forest Preserve shall be forever kept as wild forest lands. They shall not be sold, nor shall they be leased or taken, by any corporation public or private." The bill also set penalties for deliberate burning of state lands, provided for the creation of a forest warden position and hiring of inspectors, and required railroads to cut brush along their rights-of-way and to equip locomotives with spark arrestors.

One of the reasons many Adirondack residents opposed the preserve was the loss of tax dollars with great tracts of land tied up in public ownership. So in 1886, the legislature passed a law stating that forest preserve lands would be "assessed and taxed at a like valuation and at a like rate as those at which similar lands of individuals within such counties are assessed and taxed." But many towns went beyond the "like valuation" clause and taxed state lands at a higher rate than adjacent private lands, an imbalance that occurs today.

Creation of the Forest Preserve had little impact at first. Many loggers continued to cut on state lands and, if caught, merely paid the going stumpage price for the timber removed. Often they paid nothing. Because most local residents resented the Forest Preserve in the first place, they were loath to report any wrong-doing to the state. Convictions of loggers by local courts and juries were nearly impossible to obtain.

THE ADIRONDACK BLUE LINE

Reacting to this continued abuse and a growing national interest in conservation, the Forest Commission published a map in 1890 that showed most of the Adirondack region encircled in a blue line proposed as the boundary of a new state park. The purpose of the line was to delineate the general area where land purchases would be added to existing public tracts. It is doubtful the commission knew it at the time, but the region within the Blue Line represents an entire ecosystem or bioregion. To date no other single land designation in the country comes as close as the Adirondack Park in delineating the naturally existing boundaries of a major ecological unit.

With the general borders marked off, the state set about acquiring the parcels necessary to complete the proposed park. But competition for Adirondack lands was rising. More and more, wealthy individuals or groups of individuals were buying up large tracts of land for private hunting and fishing preserves. For example, in 1890, the Adirondack League Club, comprising 500 wealthy and socially prominent individuals,

Above: The Forest Commission published a map in 1890 with a blue line around the proposed park area, and the state then began to acquire privately-held lands within it.
Facing page: Cascade Falls in the Pigeon Lake Wilderness. Protection of scenic beauty was an idea new to a nation with seemingly unlimited natural resources. GEORGE WUERTHNER PHOTOS

To date no other single land designation in the country comes as close as the Adirondack Park in delineating the naturally existing boundaries of a major ecological unit.

Above: *Boat at Adirondack Museum Blue Mountain Lake.*
CLYDE SMITH
Top: *Chapel Pond.* JERI WRIGHT

purchased 104,000 acres of lake and forest country—which they promptly closed to public access.

The interest of mostly wealthy New Yorkers in the Adirondacks for recreational purposes led to accusations that the creation of the forest preserve was taking jobs away from the working man and creating a publicly financed playground for the elite and wealthy. An editor of the Warrensburg News characterized this feeling: "This whole idea of shutting so many hundred thousand acres of valuable timber lands which has and does constitute one of the chief sources of industry and commerce in the state for the enjoyment of a few wealthy politicians and summer tourists would be a serious mistake....When we consider the amount of employment afforded by the lumber industry, the thousands of saw mills, tanneries, pulp and paper mills and factories of all kinds giving labor to the hundreds of thousands of poor people and that all this is to be stopped to afford a deer park and fishing ground for a few wealthy pleasure-seekers to air their smoke-dried anatomies is an injustice, the boldness of which is astonishing."

Despite the objections of many Adirondack residents, the legislature passed the Adirondack Park Enabling Act in 1892. It designated all public lands within the Blue Line, some 681,000 acres, to be "forever reserved....for the free use of all the people." The Forest Commission, which had penciled the Blue Line had originally proposed that the state buy up all private lands within the region and consolidate public ownership into one park. This goal was never realized, so that today the term Forest Preserve refers only to state-owned lands, while Adirondack Park refers to both state and private lands within the Blue Line.

MORE CONTROVERSY

But the following year, Governor Roswell P. Flower signed yet another law that authorized the sale of timber from any part of the Forest Preserve, including the newly created park. Verplanck Colvin and the New York Board of Trade and Transportation strongly objected. The next year, Flowers would proudly announce that 17,468 acres of timber had been sold for an estimated $53,400.

To many who had fought for preservation of the forests, this timber sale represented a breach of faith. But there were to be other scandals as well. For example, when a railroad company applied for permission to build a new track across state preserve lands, those railroad commissioners who were in favor of the application called a special vote while known anti-railroad members were out of town. They sent a train to pick up one of the pro-railroad members and bring him to the meeting so he could cast his vote in favor of the line.

Those who had worked so hard to protect the Adirondack forests felt betrayed, but in 1894, they saw an opportunity to do something once and for all to preserve the mountains. A constitutional convention was meeting in Albany that year and the Board of Trade drafted an amendment to the state's constitution that would prohibit the sale of timber on preserve lands. In the final legislative shuffle the phrasing was changed slightly, but significantly to say: "Nor shall the timber thereon [on preserve lands] be sold, removed or destroyed." The delegates approved the clause, Article VII, Section 7, by a 112-0 vote and it became part of a new state constitution. The voters of New York approved the new constitution that November and the "Forever Wild" clause was given constitutional protection.

There are only two sentences in Article VII, but it is the strongest conservation protection afforded any land in the country. To make any modification to the clause requires approval of two successive sessions of the legislature, and then the new amendment must be approved by a state-wide

election. Even so, exceptions to the Forever Wild clause have been approved: the highway to the summit of Whiteface Mountain required the cutting of timber in 1927 for the right-of-way. The New York voters approved this exception and a number of others where it was obvious that the greatest public good would be realized. But the Forever Wild clause is not vulnerable to the whims of a particular governor or legislative assembly and this is what makes it unique among conservation efforts in the world.

Almost as soon as the constitution was accepted by the voters, opponents of the Forever Wild clause had drafted an amendment to undo Article VII, Section 7. The proposed changes would have allowed sale and exchange of Forest Preserve lands and, in addition, called for the lease of five-acre cottage and cabin sites. The bill was passed by two successive legislative assemblies, but voters defeated the referendum in November 1896 by a two-to-one margin.

In order to ensure that further political maneuvering would not jeopardize the goals of the Forever Wild clause, citizen watchdog groups sprang up. One of the first, formed in 1901, was the Association for the Protection of the Adirondacks, which included many of New York's most influential men such as J.P. Morgan, Alfred Vanderbilt, William Rockefeller and Louis Marshall. Later, other groups, such as the Adirondack Mountain Club (founded 1922) and Adirondack Council (1975) were organized with much the same purpose.

The Bog River near Tupper Lake.
GEORGE WUERTHNER

The Forever Wild clause is not vulnerable to the whims of a particular governor or legislative assembly and so is unique among conservation efforts in the world.

ADIRONDACK HAMLETS

Saranac Lake originally was a treatment center for tuberculosis patients. JAMES RANDKLEV

Facing page: *Cross-country skiers on Whiteface Mountain near Lake Placid. Once, summer was the only tourist season, but increasingly the Adirondacks are becoming a year-round playland.* CLYDE SMITH

In the Adirondacks and in much of New England, the word town has a slightly different meaning than it does elsewhere. It is a shortened version of township, which does not necessarily have any human population, and in the Adirondacks, some towns have very low populations indeed. The areas occupied by housing and serving as community centers are called hamlets or villages. Thus the village of Lake Placid is partially within the town of North Elba.

There are no cities within the Adirondacks and the largest hamlets are Saranac Lake, Lake Placid, Lake George Village, Tupper Lake and Old Forge. None of these "villages" exceeds 6,000 permanent residents.

Saranac Lake has perhaps the largest year-round population of any Adirondack village and, unlike other Adirondack towns, it owes its beginnings not to tourism, but to its reputation as a health resort. In the late 1800s, it was believed that exposure to the resinous odors of pines and firs would arrest or cure tuberculosis.

The physician who made Saranac Lake famous as a tuberculosis treatment center was Dr. Pierre Trudeau. Trudeau contracted TB and came to Paul Smith's resort to die in surroundings he loved. But instead of dying, Trudeau regained his health. After losing a brother and two children to the disease, he decided to spend the rest of his life trying to find a cure for tuberculosis. In 1882, he opened a research laboratory in Saranac Lake and two years later he founded the Adirondack Cottage Sanatorium in a one-room red house. He treated two patients in its first year. This house can still be seen on the grounds of the Trudeau Institute. Following this small beginning, other sanatoriums were opened near Saranac Lake including Stonywold, Gabriels and Will Rogers. By the 1920s, more than 2,000 tuberculosis patients lived in the Saranac Lake area. As part of the cure, patients spent many hours outdoors, and big screened porches lined with rocking chairs became a Saranac Lake tradition.

Just after WWI the Veterans Administration wanted to build a major hospital facility somewhere in the Adirondacks and Saranac Lake was chosen as the site. Local doctors, fearing competition from the new facility, defeated the idea. The new hospital, known as Sunmount, instead was built in Tupper Lake. The sanatorium industry fell on hard times after a cure for tuberculosis was discovered. Trudeau Sanatorium closed in 1954, although research on pulminary diseases continues to this day at the Trudeau Institute.

Besides the Trudeau Institute, Saranac Lake also

is home to the Alton Jones Cell Science Center and North Country Community College. Both broaden the economic base beyond tourism, which now is the major industry in the community. The New York State correctional facility in near-by Ray Brook is another major employer in town.

Although the village of Saranac Lake is close to lower Saranac Lake, many visitors are surprised to learn that the lake bordering the town is not one of the Saranac Lakes. It is called Lake Flowers, named for a former New York governor.

Just west of Saranac Lake is Tupper Lake. Located north of the lake that gives the town its name, Tupper Lake owes its early beginnings to the logging trade. A number of mills processed Adirondack timber here, and lumberjacks were a common sight in the town's bars. Even until 30 years ago, more than three major wood products manufacturers were located in the community, making everything from milled lumber to the wooden spoons used by a generation of kids to eat their ice cream. Today, only Veneer Hardwood still exists, but the void has been filled by other employers including

O.W.D. Plastics, Big Tupper Lake ski area, local government and the tourist service industry. But the single largest employer is the Sunmount Hospital, which currently employs some 1,000 people.

A growing problem for many Adirondack communities is garbage disposal, and Tupper Lake is no exception—its present land fill is nearly used up.

Unlike Tupper Lake, Lake Placid is not located on its namesake lake, but rather on Mirror Lake—across which Whiteface Mountain and other lofty Adirondack peaks can be seen. Lake Placid was almost from the beginning a resort town. In 1852, Nash's Red House, an old farmhouse, began to take in visitors during the summer months, and gradually the tourist trade grew. In 1895, the Lake Placid Club was started, and in 1904 introduced winter sports to the region. Ultimately this led to the selection of the town as the site for 1932 Winter Olympic Games.

The town has been an Olympic-team producer for decades beginning in 1924, when a Lake Placid resident, Charles Jewtraw, won the first Gold Medal for the 500-meter speed skating event.

Since then, the community has produced more than 60 winter Olympic contestants.

In 1980, Lake Placid again hosted the winter Olympics. In preparation, 90- and 70-meter ski jumps were built, along with a luge run on Mt. Van Hoevenberg. New ski runs and lifts on Whiteface Mountain and renovation of the Olympic Arena brought new life to the community. Today these facilities serve as an Olympic training center.

Besides employment

related to the Olympic center, some residents work at the state government facilities at Ray Brook, which include offices for APA, DEC, and the state correctional facility.

But far and away the largest employer is tourism. In 1986, more than 3 million tourists jammed Lake Placid's streets. This tourist boom has brought about a housing boom. Housing permits are up 175 percent since 1982 and more than 200 hotel

units were built in the late 1980s. Housing prices have risen by 35 percent in the last two years. Although the Adirondack Park Authority regulates development over most of the park, it has no authority to zone or direct development within established communities and Lake Placid has been caught off guard by its new popularity. There is virtually no regulation or development in the village or town of North Elba.

Lake Placid is not alone in the development boom. Another community facing similar problems is Lake George Village. Situated at the south end of the 32-mile-long lake of the same name, Lake George Village's proximity to Albany and downstate population centers has made it the first hamlet to feel the impact of escalating demands in the region. Development in the village, and in other lakeside communities like Bolton, threatens the lake itself.

Lake George was renowned for its clarity and purity, but soil erosion, septic wastes, agricultural fertilizers, herbicides and other land-based pollutants are washing into the lake and threaten the water body's very existence. Research has indicated oxygen depletion from excessive organic loading in and near Lake George's Million Dollar Beach.

Since 1975, more than 2,000 new dwellings have been built along the lake's shores, most during the mid-1980s. In 1985, 43 hotel units were constructed in Lake George and, in 1986, this more than doubled to 99 new units. Such new development often strains the old sewer facilities serving towns like Lake George.

But the problem of water pollution is related to existing buildings more often than to new ones. Year-round residences renovated from summer camps and cabins with inadequate septic systems leech pollution into the lake.

Crowding of highways, noise from an estimated 10,000 power boats on the lake during an average summer day and congestion in shopping areas threaten the peaceful serene life people seek when they vacation here.

But not everyone is dismayed by the recent boom. Long troubled by a seasonal economy and little opportunity, the Lake George area, like the rest of the Adirondacks, was crying for new jobs. And as in the rest of the Adirondacks, many residents believe zoning for wilderness values will hamper their economic future.

Proponents of zoning argue that doing nothing will eventually destroy the lake, and they argue that unbridled development could kill the goose that lays the golden egg. It is ironic that, despite the most advanced land-use zoning laws and the best attempt at planning ever attempted, the Adirondacks still might suffer degradation as a result of unwise and inappropriate development.

Above: *Hikers on Mt. Algonquin.*
Left: *Trail sign, Mt. Marcy.*

Facing page: *The confluence of East and Main Branches of the Sacandaga River, with the rolling hills of Siamese Pond Wilderness beyond.* GEORGE WUERTHNER PHOTOS

It was the automobile, coupled with growing leisure time, that brought the Adirondack Park within reach of the average American on the eastern seaboard.

Right: Sargent Ponds Wild Forest seen from Castle Rock.
Top: Little Red House was the original Trudeau tuberculosis sanitorium at Saranac Lake.

Facing page: Fresh snowfall on maple in the Saranac Lake Wild Forest.
GEORGE WUERTHNER PHOTOS

The state continued to acquire new lands, mostly parcels that logging companies no longer wanted. To avoid having to pay taxes on them, the timber companies gladly sold them to the state. New York voters continued their support by approving bond issues in 1916, 1924, 1960, 1972 and 1986 for acquisition of new additions to the Forest Preserve.

It was the automobile, however, coupled with growing leisure time, that brought the Adirondack Park within reach of the average American on the eastern seaboard. The state responded by building a number of public campgrounds and trails; in 1923, the Conservation Commission noted that more than 100,000 people had used the four state campgrounds that summer.

The popularity of such resort towns as Saranac Lake and Lake Placid continued to grow, and the development of winter sports helped to lengthen the tourist season. The 1932 Olympics were held at Lake Placid and, in 1941, ski runs were built on Whiteface Mountain, giving added impetus to the year-round tourist development.

As strong as the Forever Wild language seemed to be, it was not inflexible. Besides allowing creation of the Whiteface Mountain Highway, other exceptions have been granted through the years, including expansion of titanium mining at Tahawus, which was declared essential to the war effort during World War II. The federal government cleared the way for a railroad extension to the mine, and got an easement to 220 acres of land under the National Emergency Act, despite the Forever Wild clause. But when the war was over, the federal government extended the easement for 20 more years. Then, in 1962, it used its power of eminent domain to condemn land for a 100-year easement. The mining operations polluted the upper Hudson and eliminated Lake Sanford, which was drained and then mined. Conservationists wondered aloud whether any of this was in keeping with the spirit of the Forever Wild clause.

The mining expansion at Tahawus was just one of many controversies surrounding the interpretation of the Forever Wild doctrine. In 1950, a huge windstorm blew down timber on more than 400,000 acres of both private and public lands in the park. The Conservation Department determined that the downed timber, although a completely natural event, posed a fire hazard, and they wanted to salvage the timber in the affected areas. The state attorney general agreed with the department and a bill to allow logging within the Forest Preserve was presented to the Legislature, which approved it.

A third controversy evolved over the building of the Adirondack Northway. Supporters of the highway maintained that a superhighway was in the public interest, hence clearing of Forest Preserve lands was appropriate. Opponents countered that all kinds of development could be justified in the "public interest," including dams, ski areas, power lines and highways. Where would it stop? they asked. Eventually a compromise in route selection was reached, so that it was necessary only to clear 300 acres. Voters approved the project in 1959.

REGULATION

Despite these small intrusions into the sanctity of the Forest Preserve, during the 1960s and early 1970s, conservationists were much more worried about development on private lands over which they had no control. With the affluence realized after World War II, an even greater number of people came to the Adirondack region. In 1952, an estimated 700,000 people visited the Adirondacks but, by 1968, this number had risen to more than 8 million people. New highways like the Adirondack Northway helped speed even more people into the mountains. By the early 1970s, the Adirondacks were within a day's drive for one third of the U.S. population and two thirds of the Canadian population. The growing affluence of both countries spawned a great demand for vacation homes and other developments. Since more than 60 percent of the Adirondacks was privately owned, subdivisions, hotels, restaurants, and other facilities sprang up to satisfy the demand. Some people grumbled that success might ruin the very values that had made the Adirondacks unique. While development in the proper place might be appropriate, many felt that inappropriate, unsightly and tacky development soon would be sprawling beyond the towns, and subdivisions would invade pristine lakeshores and rural landscapes. Water, noise and visual pollution threatened the purity of the wildlands.

The patchwork of private lands interspersed among public holdings seemed to be the biggest threat to the Adirondacks' future preservation. Responding to this perception in 1967, Laurance Rockefeller, brother of New York Governor Nelson Rockefeller, proposed the creation of a 2-million-acre Adirondack National Park. Rockefeller reasoned that only the federal government had the financial ability to buy up all the private land tracts separating the numerous public parcels and to unify the Adirondacks into one great wilderness.

The APA produced a State Land Master Plan that divided the public lands into seven different use categories: wilderness, primitive, wild forest, intensive use, travel corridors, canoe, and wild and scenic rivers.

East of Blue Mountain. Less than half the park is publicly owned, and differences in land use often make it difficult to tell where boundary lines are. PETER AND ROSINE LEMMON

some of the best timberlands were to be included in the park boundaries. Many private land owners, knowing they had a good thing with their properties adjacent to large public holdings, did not want to give up these advantages or be restricted to the three-acre inholdings called for in the proposal. Finally, many residents felt the present state park already was too restrictive and they worried that a federal park would be even more so. Even preservation groups did not support the proposal, since many believed that protection afforded by the state constitution would not be guaranteed under federal administration. They believed the integrity of the Forever Wild clause might well be compromised.

While the national park idea did not get anywhere, it did raise the issue of land-use planning. Responding to these concerns, the governor appointed a Temporary Study Commission in 1966. Two years later the commission released its conclusions: The esthetic beauty of the park was threatened. The commission reported that, "The private owner of a lovely Adirondack shoreline property may now, if he likes, build on its shores a movie theater or an amusement center or a trailer park. Whatever else a movie theater or a housing development might mean, it was not in accordance with wilderness beauty." The commission recommended a radical proposal—the regulation of all lands within the Blue Line, both public and private—and proposed that a single agency be created with authority to recommend and enforce such land use management. As might be expected, any proposal to curtail individual rights, no matter how much it might protect public rights, was a highly explosive subject.

ADIRONDACK PARK AGENCY

By June of 1971, the Legislature had approved the creation of the Adirondack Park Agency (APA) to begin a unified management of all lands within the Blue Line. The APA produced a State Land Master Plan that divided the public lands into seven different use categories: wilderness, primitive, wild forest, intensive use, travel corridors, canoe, and wild and scenic rivers.

The majority of these lands was in two main categories—wilderness, which takes in 43 percent of the state lands, and wild forest, which involves 53 percent. Both classifications would maintain the ecological integrity of the landscape. Wilderness was the most restrictive category, not permitting use of any motorized vehicles or development of any kind. The APA recommended 15 wilderness areas that

Rockefeller's idea was almost universally opposed. Many residents disapproved only because it proposed to radically change the region's character, and many were uncomfortable with altering the status quo. In addition, hunters feared that a park would prohibit their sport. Lumbermen objected, since

encompassed nearly a million acres. In addition, one 18,000-acre canoe area was established, which differed little from a wilderness. Primitive areas were smaller tracts that planners thought could someday be added to the wilderness system, but which at present had some non-conforming value such as existing buildings. These totaled 78,000 acres. Finally the remaining 1 million acres of state lands were designated as wild forests, which were similar to wilderness but allowed some motorized access such as snowmobile use in winter. A few small areas were designated for intensive use, such as campgrounds, boat ramps, or ski areas.

But the APA did not limit its classification to public lands. The 3.5 million acres of private lands within the park came under a separate plan. In 1973, the APA completed the Adirondack Park Land Use and Development Plan, which divided *private* lands within the Blue Line into six categories based upon present land use and physical characteristics such as watershed, soil, vegetation and topography. As might be expected, the plan was opposed by many Adirondack residents who did not like anyone telling them what they could or could not do with their property.

The plan had to be approved by the legislature, and Adirondack representatives Glen Harris and Ronald Stafford offered a bill to delay for one year any vote on the plan. The Legislature approved it, but Governor Rockefeller, believing speed was essential to prevent further degradation of the Adirondacks, vetoed the bill. Political horse-trading followed, and a modified bill was approved. Among other things, the new version established a Local Government Review Board to advise and monitor the agency. As might be expected, the Review Board, having mostly anti-APA Adirondack residents, has an interest in obstructing agency actions that might infringe on property owners' rights.

Despite the drawbacks of the new bill, the essential elements were intact. Rather than stop all development within the park, the plan proposed to monitor and guide development to maintain essential Adirondack qualities such as scenic beauty, and open space.

The most flexible category in terms of land use is that of "Hamlet," which recognizes the existing settlements. No restrictions on intensity of development are imposed and in fact, the plan recommended future growth be concentrated in these areas.

Other divisions include Industrial Use, where factories or mining are allowed, then in descending order of impact of

pre-existing development are Moderate Intensity Use, Low Intensity Use and Rural Use. These are primarily areas where homes can be built. Finally, the most restrictive private land use category is Resource Management. Here development is limited to 15 buildings per square mile, for an average lot size of 42.6 acres.

Allowing for an average lot size proved a very large loophole. The law does not prescribe *where* within the one square mile those 15 buildings should be built, so in some cases, houses are clustered along lakeshores leaving the rest of the acreage undeveloped. Since one intent of the law was to prevent the build-up of lakeshore property in pristine areas, this compromises the intent of the law.

These drawbacks were accepted as necessary and the New York Legislature approved the bill's new version. On May 22, 1973, Governor Rockefeller signed it into law.

But to many Adirondack area residents the new plan was an unwanted intrusion into their lives. Criticizing the APA became a favorite form of rural entertainment and tempers flashed as the young agency attempted to implement sections of the plan. Adirondack residents were aroused and began to organize to defend their interests. William Doolittle, at the time publisher of the *Adirondack Daily Enterprise*,

Above: *Canoe on a misty lake.* PETER LEMMON **Top:** *Dock on Lake Placid. According to APA regulations, most development is confined to existing centers, such as Lake Placid.* GEORGE WUERTHNER

Above: *Dawn on Lake Champlain.*
ALBERT GATES
Right: *Wind surfer at Lake George.*
GEORGE WUERTHNER

To many Adirondack area residents the new plan was an unwanted intrusion.

summed up the feelings of many residents when he expressed his displeasure with the APA's zoning restrictions. "The people of the state did not have the will to buy up all the private land in the park, so the APA simply took it."

At the heart of the issue of the APA controversy is what is known as "the taking clause" in the Fifth Amendment of the United States Constitution, which guarantees that private property cannot be taken for public use, "without just compensation." Opponents of regional land-use planning and regulation filed lawsuits amounting to nearly $50 million in the first two years of the APA's existence, largely based upon this clause.

Opponents of zoning argue that it prevents the owner from developing it to his or her maximum advantage, effectively taking away the property. For example, those owning property in the Resource Management zone might argue that since that specific zoning classification limits development to just 15 principal buildings per square mile, anyone wishing to build a hundred houses on that acreage is theoretically losing certain options to maximize profits. Proponents of zoning claim that the government has not physically taken away the property, but merely limited what can be done there.

The Adirondacks, of course, are not the only place where zoning has come under attack, and there have been many cases seeking to clarify just exactly what constitutes "taking" and what does not. A recent U.S. Supreme Court case made some Adirondack residents optimistic that they will be able to invalidate the APA's land-use plan. The case involved a church group in California, which had built a camp in the flood plain of a narrow canyon. A flood washed away the camp, and the county government would not permit the church to rebuild due to the obvious flood danger. The church sued the county saying that, in effect, the county had taken away their property. The Supreme Court decided that the church was entitled to monetary compensation—if the courts determine that it has been deprived of *all use of its land*.

That is the critical language that APA officials say will save them. Their zoning ordinances do not limit all uses, only some—such as housing-unit density on a particular parcel. Nevertheless, the Local Review Board presently is planning a lawsuit to challenge the APA's regulations and will argue that all affected residents are entitled to some compensation.

Despite what appears to be fairly strict regulation of development, preservationists point out that under the present laws nearly a half a million new houses still can be built within the park.

To the occasional visitor, it may seem ironic that Adirondack residents, who can enjoy the park year-round, have fought APA regulations so consistently. Proponents of APA argue that individuals stifled by regulations have ample opportunity for unlimited development in the rest of the state. But in this one exquisite place, a line has been drawn. Here, development will be done differently, with more care, with more forethought and with sensitivity to the landscape. It is a way of living *with* the earth rather than merely on it.

Right: *Paper birches along Thirteenth Lake, Siamese Pond Wilderness.* GEORGE WUERTHNER
Below: *Canoes at sunset, Middle Saranac Lake.*
JERI WRIGHT

ROBERT MARSHALL

Robert Marshall died at 38 of a heart attack while riding a train from Washington to New York. It was an ironic end for a man who thought nothing of hiking 40 or more miles in a single day and who, in that short lifetime, fit in more living than most people achieve in twice as many years. While still in college, he and his brother George—along with guide Herb Clark—climbed all 46 Adirondack peaks above 4,000′, becoming the first "46ers" in Adirondack history. (More precise surveys have shown that the original measurements were off a bit and there are actually only 43 peaks at or above 4,000′.)

Deciding that life in the outdoors was the only suitable option for himself, Marshall studied forestry at New York School of Forestry at Syracuse University, where he graduated with honors. Later he received a Ph.D. in plant physiology from Johns Hopkins University. He eventually found employment with the U.S. Forest Service and Bureau of Indian Affairs—positions that gave him ample opportunity to personally explore many western roadless areas. His last position was as chief of the U.S. Forest Service's Divi-

sion of Recreation and Lands, where he worked vigorously toward the creation of primitive areas— an administrative designation used by the Forest Service before passage of the 1964 Wilderness Act.

Marshall used every spare day to get in a hike or two in these wild regions and these explorations often turned into marathon 40-mile-a-day treks. Before he died he had explored much of northern Alaska, and proposed a national park in the Gates of the Arctic region of Alaska's Brooks Range.

Between work and hikes, he found time to write articles, two books (and part of a third), including one in which he called for the public ownership of all forests. For this and many other liberal views, he was listed by a House Committee on Un-American activities as a possible communist. Marshall was under investigation by the FBI and he was twice

Right: A youthful Bob Marshall.
Facing page: Looking to High Peaks from Giant Mountain across St. Hubert's. Bob Marshall, with his brother George and guide Herb Clark, were the first to climb all Adirondack peaks above 4,000 feet. GEORGE WUERTHNER

Above: *Hikers on Pitchoff Mountain.* CLYDE SMITH
Facing page: High Falls on the Oswegatchie River, now part of the Five Ponds Wilderness. This is one of the areas Marshall explored and grew to love. The Five Ponds Wilderness is part of a proposed 160,000-acre Bob Marshall Wilderness. GEORGE WUERTHNER

investigated by Congress for his radical political stands.

But there is no doubt that Marshall loved his country—perhaps better than those who accused him of un-American attitudes, for he was constantly trying to preserve the American landscape so that future Americans would know the joys of wild country.

Just before his untimely death, he had formed The Wilderness Society, which today is one of the most effective conservation organizations in the United States. Somehow, with all these travels and responsibilities, he always found time to return to his first love—the Adirondacks.

Born in 1901, the son of Louis Marshall, a wealthy New York lawyer and a strong supporter of the Forever Wild clause protecting the Adirondacks, Bob Marshall literally grew up in the Adirondacks. His family owned Camp Knollwood on Lower Saranac Lake where they spent their summers. Always a romantic, young Marshall dreamed of being an explorer in the mold of Lewis and Clark, but he thought he had been born too late for genuine exploration. Then one summer he discovered some dusty copies of Verplanck Colvin's survey reports, which described Colvin's explorations of the Adirondacks during the 1870s and 1880s. Colvin's books fired young Marshall's imagination, and he proposed to his younger brother George that they should attempt to duplicate Colvin's explorations.

Bob was 15 and George 12, when they accompanied the family guide Herb Clark, and climbed their first Adirondack peak—Ampersand Mountain. The experience was addictive, and the Marshall boys began to plan their summers around hiking and climbing. Two years later, they climbed Whiteface Mountain, their first 4,000-footer. During the succeeding summers they would eventually climb every peak over 4,000' and Bob described these climbs in his booklet, "High Peaks of the Adirondacks," which was published in 1922. In it, Bob also rated the view from each peak, placing Haystack as the best considering scenic qualities, wildness and other characteristics. Santanoni was second while Nye placed last.

Marshall was also a fanatic about statistics and record keeping—particularly as it pertained to his hiking and climbing adventures. One hike in July of 1932 is typical. Marshall set out at 3:30 in the morning to begin his hike and by 10:30 that evening, he had completed his "day," chalking up 14 peaks and ascending, by his own calculation, some 13,600'.

After many trips in the West, Marshall was back at Knollwood and after climbing eight peaks in one day—routine for this greyhound of a hiker—he confided to a friend: "...in spite of the more rugged mountains in a few parts of the west, the Adirondacks are still my favorites, and so the day was glorious." In fact, the very first issue of The Wilderness Society's journal *Living Wilderness* (September 1935), included a letter Marshall had written to New York Conservation Commissioner Lithgow Osborne, pleading for preservation of three large roadless areas in the Adirondacks.

Marshall is commemorated by Mt. Marshall in the High Peaks. But today there is a motion to honor this wilderness visionary further by reviving Marshall's dream of a giant Adirondack wilderness in the region south of Cranberry Lake. The Adirondack Council is advocating an Adirondack Bob Marshall Wilderness (there is already a federally designated Bob Marshall Wilderness in Montana), which would include the existing Five Ponds and Pepperbox Wilderness plus adjacent private land.

As Marshall pleaded 50 years ago: "There is just one hope of repulsing the tyrannical ambition of civilization to conquer every niche on the whole earth. That hope is the organization of spirited people who will fight for the freedom of wilderness." Perhaps Bob Marshall's greatest legacy is that he has inspired a generation of Americans to work towards just that end.

THE FUTURE OF THE ADIRO

Skier at sunset. CLYDE SMITH

DEVELOPMENT

A building boom is on in the Adirondacks. In 1987 building permits were up 35 percent over previous years and many believe the present legislation, though containing the strongest zoning laws in the nation, is too lax. Among the proposed developments within park boundaries are 92 condominiums in Lake George, 150 townhouses in Bolton, 182 townhouses in Speculator, 100 condominiums in Schroon Lake. Up to a half million new dwellings can be built within the park even under the existing restrictions, and this, say park preservationists, poses a great threat to the region's scenic qualities, water and other natural resources. Lake George, for example, already is showing serious degradation of its once-pristine waters due to leaky and faulty septic systems that are polluting the lake.

This development boom has other consequences for the future of the park. In 1986 alone, the price of land skyrocketed 30 percent above the previous year's values, making state acquisition more expensive and more difficult. The rising land prices also make subdivision and sale of the large land parcels owned by timber companies more lucrative and attractive. For example, International Paper Company, which owns 300,000 acres in the Adirondacks, has begun to sell some of its lands to developers.

The Adirondack Park is a glorious experiment. With legislation and money, the people of New York are working toward recreating a wilderness ecosystem from fragmented parcels of the original whole. Can the state outbid the developers for land; will the zoning laws ultimately hold up in court?

ACQUISITION

First, many conservationists are working towards greater public ownership, though most have accepted the idea that total public control of the area within the Blue Line probably will be impossible, if for no other reason than that it would be prohibitively expensive to purchase all those inholdings. Some of the more moderate proposals call for a 50-50 proportion of private to public ownership, assuming the state can outbid developers who often are after the same parcels.

No matter how much land eventually is acquired, purchasing will aim for key private parcels to round out ecological units or potential recreational sites. For example, procurement of a canoe right-of-passage around private lands at Split Rock Falls on the Bog River would open a 69-mile canoe route between Saranac Lake and Oswegatchie River. Other purchases would be targeted towards rounding out biological diversity. In this group would be currently private holdings in the northwest portion of the park in the St. Regis, Jordan and lower Raquette River drainages, which would ensure adequate representation of the low-elevation boreal forest ecosystem.

Additions to existing state lands could help to complete ecological units. George Davis, a planner for the Adirondack Council, outlines creation of a West Canada Lakes Ecological Wilderness of more than 250,000 acres delineated by watershed boundaries rather than property lines. His plan would combine additions to the existing West Canada Lake Wilderness (including the upper portion of the West Canada Creek drainage basin upstream from Nobleboro), along with reclassification of the South Fork of the Moose River from

The Adirondack Park is a glorious experiment.

Second Pond in Saranac Lake system.
GEORGE WUERTHNER

85

Crowfoot Pond. ALBERT GATES

If the DEC continues to target its purchases and the development of private grounds can be contained, no doubt the Adirondacks will become wilder, and ecologically more sound, than today.

wild forest to wilderness, and also with purchase of privately-held parcels in the Cedar River Flow and near Buell Brook.

Davis also has a similar vision for consolidation of public and private holdings in the High Peaks area, which would add lands to the south along the upper Hudson River and upper Boreas River drainages, including the North Branch of the Boreas. In addition, the Dix Mountain Wilderness would be added to the High Peaks Wilderness, resulting in a 330,000-acre ecological wilderness.

CLASSIFICATION

But land acquisition is not the only area of concern for Adirondack supporters. In some ways they advocate changing land classification status to preserve natural features. For example, there are 1,238 miles of state-designated Wild, Scenic and Recreational Rivers within the Adirondack Park, but another 97 miles have been recommended for classification and protection. In addition to preventing the construction of dams, designation does restrict some types of construction and development. A creative option being advocated is

construction of trail systems to parallel these rivers, providing a recreational opportunity presently unavailable in much of the park.

In addition to these measures designed to protect ecosystems, conservationists also propose protection of scenic highway corridors. At present some 89 percent of the roadsides in the park are privately owned and could eventually be developed to some extent. One solution is to buy conservation easements along these routes, and keep the roadsides in an undeveloped state.

With protection and consolidation of holdings, the restoration of extinct native species is possible. The moose may be recolonizing the region on its own, while others (like the lynx) are to be reintroduced. Other species that may find a home in the Adirondacks include mountain lion and wolf.

RESTORATION

Finally, conservationists are interested in a restoration of natural ecological processes, whether that entails letting the occasional lightning-caused fire burn thousands of acres,

or allowing disease or a harsh winter to reduce deer herds. An ecosystem without these periodic disruptions will fail as a naturally-balanced ecosystem, and restoration of the Adirondacks is tied to protecting all natural *processes* as well as species.

The people of New York State have indicated their strong support for the goals and purpose of the park by passing a $250 million bond issue in 1986 to provide for, among other things, additional land acquisition. In 1986, the Department of Environmental Conservation (DEC) purchased 33,266 acres at an average cost of $186 each. One of the most important acquisitions was the Watson's East Triangle, which adjoins the Five Ponds and Pepperbox wildernesses. This purchase will enable the consolidation of two separate wildernesses, making the Bob Marshall State Wilderness a reality.

If the DEC continues to target its purchases and the development of private grounds can be contained, no doubt the Adirondacks will become wilder, and ecologically more sound, than today. New York State will have done what even federal governments largely failed to do—create a functioning ecosystem from a fragmented whole.

Left: *Birch leaf on moss.*
Top right: *Indian Falls, High Peaks Wilderness.*
Top left: *Lake Clear near Paul Smiths.* GEORGE WUERTHNER PHOTOS

GUIDE TO WILD AREAS

Above: *Fall color of maples along the Ausable River.* JAMES RANDKLEV
Right: *Ferns in a Five Ponds Wilderness forest.* GEORGE WUERTHNER

Facing page: *Oswegatchie River, Five Ponds Wilderness.* GEORGE WUERTHNER

WILDERNESS AREAS*

Blue Ridge Wilderness—45,736 acres. Located south of Blue Mountain Lake off Highway 28, and north of the Cedar River Flow, this wilderness is dominated by Blue Ridge, which runs east- west for more than 6 miles. At its highest point, it is 3,497' in elevation. Lower elevations are covered with mixed hardwood forest, while the highest basins and ridgetops extend into the spruce-fir zone. One of the major deer wintering areas in the region exists along Loon Brook.

A number of trout ponds can be accessed by trails, along with a portion of the Northville-Placid Trail. There is abundant beaver activity.

Dix Mountain Wilderness—45,208 acres. Located near Keene, this wilderness is immediately east of the High Peaks Wilderness and also is very mountainous, with several peaks exceeding 4,000'—including Dix Mountain itself. Vertical cliffs are common and local relief can be severe. Popular roadside areas include Chapel Pond.

Some of the worst of the turn-of-the-century forest fires burned over this region, eliminating not only trees but also the humus and mineral soil. As a result, there are extensive areas of fire-dependent forest species like paper birch and aspen. Due to the lack of mineral soil, many balsam firs at higher elevations are stunted.

There are four trailless peaks about 4,000'—South Dix, East Dix, Hough and Macomb. And these plus other peaks provide outstanding views of the High Peaks. One of the better views is from the summit of Noonmark Mountain.

Five Ponds Wilderness—101,171 acres. This wilderness is located in the western portion of the park south of Cranberry Lake. Terrain is rolling with a few scattered high hills, the

*Wilderness acreages include all purchases as of 1986.

89

highest being 2,489′ Summit Mountain. Swamps, ponds and lakes (79 of them named) and rivers such as the Oswegatchie dominate. Glacial features are common, including eskers, moraine and erratics. The Five Ponds esker is one of the best developed eskers in the Adirondacks and is identified in the State Land Master Plan as a natural special-interest area.

During the logging era, the Oswegatchie River was used to float logs to sawmills downstream. About half the present wilderness never was logged, and hence contains the largest stand of virgin timber in the Northeast. Even within logged areas, some of the trees were too big for the horse and oxen teams to haul to landings, so even here remain scattered virgin stands of spruce and white pine. One representative stand of old-growth pine can be found on an esker near Five Ponds and Wolf Pond.

Another area of botanical interest is the "The Plains," an open area of shrubby vegetation similar to the Moose River Plains south of Raquette Lake.

Although there are numerous trails, most recreational use is concentrated on the Oswegatchie River where canoeists paddle up the slow-moving river to High Falls—a spectacular setting with good fishing. The Oswegatchie with its deep undercut banks and tannin-stained, dark but clear, water is reminiscent of Alaskan tundra rivers. Many people hire canoes and camp along the shore of Cranberry Lake, one of the largest water bodies in the Adirondacks under nearly complete state ownership.

Many of the lakes south of Five Ponds now are sterile and support no fish because of acid rain. Ponds to the north are less affected and so far still contain fish.

The Five Ponds Wilderness would form the heart of the proposed Bob Marshall State Wilderness, which conservationists hope can be created by combining Five Ponds with the Pepperbox Wilderness and purchasing existing adjacent private lands.

Giant Mountain Wilderness—22,916 acres. Most people driving Highway 73 stop to admire Roaring Brook Falls, but few realize that this is part of the Giant Mountain Wilderness. A hike to the falls is easy and even a hike to the summit of Giant Mountain itself is relatively short. The views from the top are outstanding. Much of this area burned in 1903, fire consuming the humus and soils, leaving the top of the mountain practically bald. There are occasional pockets of old-growth timber that the fires missed, and these contain

large hemlocks and white pines, but the remainder of the area is covered by paper birch and other hardwoods.

Giant Mountain rises steeply from the surrounding land. In fact, the elevational difference from the eastern border of the wilderness to the top of the mountain equals 4,000′, the greatest of any of the state's wildernesses. Hiking is the

Above: *Looking south from Mt. Defiance along Lake Champlain.*

Facing page: *Horseshoe Falls in the Ausable Gorge.*
GEORGE WUERTHNER PHOTOS

predominant use. Since there are only two water bodies—Giant's Washbowl and Lake Marie Louise—little fishing occurs except along the Ausable River, which delineates one border of the area.

Ha De Ron Dah Wilderness—26,528 acres. Located in the extreme western portion of the park west of Old Forge, the Ha De Ron Dah wilderness consists of small ponds, streams, swamps and lakes amid rolling hills. About half of the 20 water bodies in this small wilderness contain fish.

Much of the southern half was burned by wildfire and has revegetated with pin cherry, aspen and bracken fern. Over the northern half, mixed hardwoods dominate, most of it second-growth timber. A few large pines exist, which were not cut when the area first was harvested.

There are a trail system and seven lean-to's but use is light and this is one area where visitors can obtain solitude rather easily.

High Peaks Wilderness—192,685 acres. This is the Adirondacks' largest—and most popular—wilderness. The trail to Mt. Marcy from Adirondak Loj via Indian Falls is one of the most heavily used in the entire park. Other high-use areas include Marcy Dam, Lake Colden, and the Johns Brook Valley. Some people complain that overuse is destroying the wilderness values in popular destinations like Lake Colden, and have proposed permits as a means of restricting use, but others favor closing access roads so that the approach is lengthened. This would make it more difficult to penetrate the heart of the region without spending at least one night on the trail.

The reasons for the popularity of this region are twofold. Access to the very heart of the this region is made easy by an excellent trail system. Even a round-trip climb to the top of the highest peaks is easily accomplished in a single day. In addition, the scenery is spectacular. Dominated by steep cliff faces and high summits, this wilderness contains most of the Adirondack peaks above 4,000′, including New York's highest summit, Mt. Marcy. This is the finest mountain area in the East.

Contrasting to the heavy use seen in the Marcy area, the region to the west along the Cold River is one of the most remote portions of the park and few people enter it.

Scenic attractions are many including the sheer walls along Avalanche Lake and Indian Pass and the numerous streams. Many, like the Opalescent River, have a multitude of falls and cascades. Finally, there is the attraction of the state's highest mountains and lakes, including Lake Tear of the Clouds—ultimate source of the Hudson River.

Vegetation is varied. Much of the area was burned around the turn of the century and is covered with a mixture of small pole-sized hardwoods, like birch, interspersed with pockets of mature timber that escaped the fire. One passes through some of this large timber on the way to Marcy Dam. At the highest elevations, alpine tundra exists, with the most extensive stands being on Marcy and Algonquin. Unfortunately, this tundra is extremely susceptible to tramping and, in many areas, human use has eliminated much of this unique vegetation zone.

Hoffman Notch Wilderness—36,305 acres. To the west of the Schroon River lie the rugged ridges that comprise the Hoffman Notch Wilderness. These ridges—Blue Ridge, Washburn Ridge and Texas Ridge—are aligned in a generally north-south direction. Hoffman Mountain is the highest point and once was proposed as a ski area, but the proposal was defeated in a referendum placed before the voters in 1967.

There are eight lakes and ponds and most use is from hunters and fishermen.

Although most of the forest cover is second-growth hardwood, as in most Adirondack locations, conifers cover the higher elevations. On the best soils, there are some very large second-growth hardwoods.

Jay Mountain Wilderness—7,100 acres. Lying northeast of Keene, the small Jay Mountain area recently was upgraded to Wilderness from Primitive status. It is a mountainous region, with Jay Mountain one of the highest elevations. From its summit, enjoy views of the Champlain Valley as well as of the High Peaks.

McKenzie Mountain Wilderness—37,616 acres. Just north of Ray Brook lies the McKenzie Mountain Wilderness. The two major topographical features are McKenzie Mountain (sometimes called Saddleback) and Moose Mountain (often called St. Armand). Both offer fine views from their summits.

After the 1950s blowdown, roads were bulldozed into this areas from both the north and south, but time has eliminated most of the scars. One of the longest log flumes in the eastern U.S. once ran from Lake Stevens to the Ausable River.

Above: *The Cedar River.* GEORGE WUERTHNER
Left: *Snapping turtle.* GERARD LEMMO

Facing page: *Boulders and red pines along Rock Pond, Pharaoh Lake Wilderness.* GEORGE WUERTHNER

Pepperbox Wilderness—14,625 acres. The Pepperbox is as wild as any place in the Adirondacks. Basically nothing more than a very wet lowland area with scattered stands of second-growth spruce, fir and red maple, it has only 2 miles of trail. Access is difficult and one wanting solitude will find it here.

The wetlands, while not beckoning the average hiker, do provide outstanding wildlife habitat. This area's most important value may be in its use as a outdoor biological laboratory.

Pepperbox, along with the Five Ponds Wilderness and adjoining private lands, is part of the 350,000-acre Bob Marshall Wilderness proposal.

Pharaoh Lake Wilderness—45,884 acres. Just east of Schroon Lake is the western boundary of the Pharaoh Lake Wilderness. Pharaoh Lake, located nearly in the center of the wilderness, is one of the largest water bodies in the Adirondack Park entirely surrounded by state lands. But here are 35 other water bodies, including Putnam Pond, connected by an extensive trail system that offers the visitor more than enough camping destinations or places to fish.

The general terrain is rolling and Pharaoh Mountain at 2,557′ is the highest peak. Pharaoh Mountain, as well as many other peaks, has been burned over and thus offers panoramic views despite their low elevation. Occasional stands of timber missed by the fires and loggers provide some high-quality hardwood groves, particularly in the northeast. The entire area was glaciated, as evidenced by erratics, barren rock points and sharp cliffs on southwest faces.

Pigeon Lake Wilderness—50,100 acres. The Pigeon Lake Wilderness lies northeast of Big Moose Lake extending from Stillwater Reservoir to Raquette Lake. Terrain is rolling, with no really high peaks, and swamplands are extensive— particularly along Sucker Brook and Beaver Brook. More than 64 lakes and ponds offer attractive destinations, though few have trail access.

Most of the region is covered with hardwood forest, but conifers dominate the wetter areas. Old-growth white pine is found near Pigeon Lake, and large old-growth yellow birch can be seen along the trail to Queer Lake.

Sentinel Range Wilderness—23,252 acres. Heading east out of Lake Placid, look to the east to see the Sentinel Range. Relief is great here and cliffs are a common feature. All of the region was burned by extensive forest fires and the forest cover is now regenerating. The Old Military Road passes through the heart of this area, and is now a hiking trail. Other than a few ponds on the northern fringes, the area receives little use. Good views can be had by climbing Pitchoff Mountain, accessible from Highway 73.

Siamese Ponds Wilderness—112,524 acres. This is the third-largest wilderness area in the Adirondacks and is located northeast of Speculator. Like much of the park, it was cut over by loggers nearly a century ago. Nevertheless, time has healed most of the damage and today the area is probably wilder than it was in the late 1800s.

Most of the terrain is rolling with a few peaks like Puffer and South Pond Mountain extending above 3,000′. The glaciers that overrode this country left some 60 to 70 ponds and lakes, with fjord-like Thirteenth Lake the largest. Thirteenth Lake has landlocked salmon, while many of the higher ponds, such as Puffer and Siamese, offer outstanding brook trout fishing. Augur Falls is a favorite hiking destination along the Main Branch of the Sacandaga River.

Silver Lake Wilderness—105,270 acres. Northwest of Great Sacandaga Lake lie the rolling hills of the Silver Lake Wilderness. This large but relatively little-used wilderness is the southern terminus of the Northville-Lake Placid Trail. Lakes like Silver, Mud, and Rock attract the fisherman, but otherwise the area is seldom visited. Swamps and beaver flows are common.

Since this region, on the southern edge of the Adirondacks and closest to the early sawmills in Glens Falls and elsewhere, was most accessible to early loggers, most of it has been cut over at some time in the past, but it was one of the first tracts acquired by the state and the forests now appear near-virgin. Nevertheless, some large-diameter hemlocks along with other mature forests give the area a pristine feel.

Above: Peaks of the Sentinel Range Wilderness, with Whiteface Mountain beyond.
Facing page, left: Nichols Brook, Sentinel Range State Wilderness.
Right: Birch trunk and maple leaves.
GEORGE WUERTHNER PHOTOS

Right: *Raquette Lake.*
GEORGE WUERTHNER

Facing page: *Clear Pond from Sunrise Mountain.*
ALBERT GATES

West Canada Lakes Wilderness—156,735 acres. Located south of the Fulton Chain Lakes, this wilderness is the second-largest roadless area in the Adirondacks (after the High Peaks region) and it is far wilder, especially since float planes were banned from landing on the interior lakes. Because of the size of this area, the major lakes like Cedar and West Canada are beyond the reach of the casual hiker and have remained relatively wild.

The region forms the headwaters for three drainage basins: Mohawk, Black and Hudson and is lake-studded (168 bodies of water), but many ponds are dying or already dead as a result of acid rain.

Terrain is rolling with numerous swamps and beaver flows, and no really high peaks.

St. Regis Canoe Area—18,563 acres. Similar to a wilderness area, the St. Regis Canoe area was designated to provide a canoe loop route in a wild setting. The St. Regis basin is a lake-studded (58 lakes) area with most ponds accessible by a short carry, making it ideal for canoe-tripping.
Fires burned over much of the area, but large white pines along the shores of some lakes escaped this fate and provide a majestic backdrop for shoreline camps.

PRIMITIVE AREAS

Primitive areas usually are unsuitable for wilderness classification for a variety of reasons, such as small size, presence of non-conforming structures and roads, etc. In total there are 64,913 acres of the park within this classification. As of 1986, they included: Ampersand, Bald Ledge, Buck Pond, Buell Brook, Cathead Mountain, Crane Pond, Dug Mountain, Fort Noble Mountain, Hudson Gorge, Hurricane Mountain, Johns Brook, Lake Lila, Pillsbury Lake, Sacandaga, Valcour Island, Wakely Mountain, West Canada Mountain, Wilmurt Club Road.

WILD FOREST AREAS

Wild Forests cover 1,227,563 acres of the Adirondack Park and thus offer substantial recreational opportunities. In many instances, the only difference between a Wild Forest and Wilderness is that the former allows some non-conforming uses such as snowmobile travel or woods roads. Many wild forests may be managed so that eventually they are upgraded to Wilderness classification. The following are brief descriptions of *some* of the larger wild forest areas.

Whiteface Mountain seen from Cherrypatch Pond.
GEORGE WUERTHNER

Black River Wild Forest—Along the western border of the park south of Old Forge lies the Black River Wild Forest. Most of the area consists of second-growth forest, with swampy areas interspersed among low hills. Many of the 36 water bodies lack fish, since the effects of acid rain have been most severe in this section of the park.

Blue Mountain Wild Forest—Located northeast of Blue Mountain Lake, this area is dominated by 3,759' Blue Mountain. One of the more popular lakes is Tirrell Pond. An unbroken 10-mile-long block of Forest Preserve land runs from East Inlet Mountain to Fishing Brook Range and is accessed by the Northville-Lake Placid trail.

Cranberry Lake Wild Forest—This area is located by Cranberry Lake in the northwestern section of the park. It offers a glimpse of the lowland boreal forest habitat, which is not well represented among state lands. Snowmobiling is a favorite activity here, although hiking is possible in summer, to a number of remote trout ponds.

Debar Mountain Wild Forest—Named for the highest mountain in this northern section of the park, the summit of Debar Mountain offers outstanding views of the High Peaks to the south. Meacham Lake campground is a popular recreation site, and fishing in the Osgood River is above average.

Ferris Lake Wild Forest—Visitors can drive through a nearly wild area and never leave the car, in the Ferris Lake Wild Forest. The dirt road between Route 10 by Piseco Lake to Stratford passes through the center of this forest and weaves among numerous ponds, lakes and streams where trout await the angler's hook. Because of the access, hunting is a popular activity in the fall.

Hammond Pond Wild Forest—This area located north of Schroon Lake offers a wide variety of forest types and lowland species like oak, ash and basswood—common on the southern, warmer exposures. Good views are possible from the many ledges and rocky outcrops, as well as from the summit of Owl Pate and Hail mountains.

Independence River Wild Forest—Just south of Stillwater Reservoir is the Independence River which drains an area of low relief that includes some sand plains. Bogs and beaver ponds are common, and important for a variety of wildlife species.

Jessup River Wild Forest—The mix of private lands, where logging occurs (providing food for big game species like deer), with public lands (providing security cover) makes this area a favorite with hunters. Both the Jessup and Miami rivers, which drain this area, are well known trout fisheries. The view from Pillsbury Mountain is outstanding.

Lake George Wild Forest—Cradling Lake George is the Lake George Wild Forest. The generally low elevation coupled with the lakes's moderating influence has allowed many plants typical of southern New York to survive in this region. Oak and pine are common, and there are many rare plant species. Here, one also will find the rare timber rattler, a species rapidly disappearing over much of its former natural range.

Despite the low overall elevation, outstanding views of Lake George are possible from Tongue Mountain and Black Mountain which, at 2,646′, is the highest mountain rimming Lake George.

Moose River Plains Wild Forest—Located south of the Fulton Chain Lakes, the Moose River Plains are not really plains in the usual sense of the word, but a rather open expanse with low shrubby vegetation and scattered trees. Numerous roads provide access to this region and camping is permitted all along these roadways.

Saranac Lakes Wild Forest—Part of the great lake-studded basin that includes all the Saranac Lakes and Tupper Lake, this region holds many interconnected waterways. Canoeing is perhaps the best way of traveling the region. Tamarack bogs are common and, in autumn, the bright golden needles add color to the region.

Sargent Ponds Wild Forest—Rolling terrain northwest of Blue Mountain Lake, this tract includes or borders the Raquette River, Marion River and Boulder Brook. Swamp and bog are common with spruce, white cedar and balsam fir throughout. Canoeing along the Marion River between Raquette Lake and Blue Mountain Lake is a popular activity.

Shaker Mountain Wild Forest—Little-used although just north of Albany and Schenectady, this region of gentle hills was heavily logged prior to state acquisition. Many roads penetrate the woodlands and offer easy hiking opportunities.

Vanderwhacker Wild Forest—The view of the High Peaks from the top of 3,386′ Vanderwhacker Mountain is considered one of the best in the Adirondacks. The Boreas River, which offers both whitewater and quiet stretches, is one of the more beautiful Adirondack rivers, much of it flowing through a landscape of boreal forest more typical of areas farther north.

Wilcox Lake Wild Forest—The number of snowmobile trails in this forest is perhaps greater than in any other portion of the park. Old logging roads are common and provide most of the foot trails. Despite past logging, there are immense trees in some areas. Numerous ponds and brooks provide fishing opportunities. In general this, like many other Wild Forest areas, is neglected by recreationists.

Above: *South Creek near Middle Saranac Lake, Saranac Lake Wild Forest.*
Left: *In Moose River Plains Wild Forest.* GEORGE WUERTHNER PHOTOS

upon the character of the land through which it flows, it is entirely possible for one river to have segments in more than one of these categories.

A river selected for designation under the Wild and Scenic Rivers Act is protected against dams and is to remain in its free-flowing condition. Regulations in the act also control development along the shoreline and limit the kinds of scenic intrusions permitted. Usually, the river corridor one quarter of a mile from each bank of the river comes under the act's regulatory powers.

The Wild and Scenic Rivers Act prohibits new hydroelectric dams on free-flowing rivers, but allows existing dam facilities to continue operation. A 1982 Adirondack Park Agency study found that park rivers contributed two percent of the state's hydro power.

Wild rivers are managed to maintain their wild character. To qualify, a river segment must be accessible by foot or canoe, with no roads nearby. It must be free-flowing and a minimum of five miles in length.
Classified as wild have been 155.1 miles of rivers, including parts of the Cedar, Cold, Hudson, Indian, Kunjamuk, Opalescent, Main and Middle Branches of the Oswegatchie, and East and West Branches of the Sacandaga, Piseco Lake Outlet, West Canada Creek, South Branch West Canada Creek, Ouluska Pass Brook.

Scenic rivers are usually of limited access, although a road occasionally may cross the stream. Forestry or other non-wilderness land uses can be practiced on adjacent lands. Utility lines cannot be visible from the river and no new development—even on private lands—is permitted within 250' of the river except for minor intrusions like docks, fences, and bridges. New houses must meet minimum setbacks to be invisible from the river corridor.

There are 517.3 miles of rivers classified as scenic. These include parts of the East Branch of the Ausable, Black, Bog, Boreas, Boquet, Cedar, Deer, Middle, South, and North Branches of the Grasse, Hudson, Independence, Jordan, Kunjamuk, Marion, Main, North and South Branches of the Moose, Middle and West Branches of the Oswegatchie, Raguette, Red, Rock, East, West and Main Branches of the St. Regis, Ampersand Brook, Otter Brook, Long Pond Outlet, Round Lake Outlet, Blue Mountain Stream, East and West Canada Creek, West Stony Creek.

WILD AND SCENIC RIVERS

New York's Wild and Scenic Rivers Act was fashioned after the federal Wild and Scenic Rivers system plan. Ninety percent of the rivers so classified are in the Adirondacks.

There are three sub-classifications, dependent primarily upon accessibility and present character of the river corridor. The most remote river segments, primarily passing through designated wilderness, are classified as Wild. Scenic rivers usually pass through land under some kind of non-wilderness land, such as timber harvest or farming country. Finally, the least restrictive classification is Recreational, which implies the river is less than pristine—a road or railroad may follow its banks, or it may have been dammed in the past. Depending

Recreational rivers have 565.9 designated miles within the Adirondacks, which are managed to preserve water quality, recreational opportunities, and scenic vistas. Although a road may be adjacent to a recreational river, utility lines must be invisible from the stream. New structures within 150' of the high-water mark are prohibited, with the exception of lean-to's, docks, bridges, and the like. Minimum set-backs apply to houses, along with lot width.

Rivers classified as recreational include: parts of the East, Main and West Branches of the Ausable, Black, Boquet, Cedar, South Branch of the Grasse, Hudson, Independence, Indian, Middle Branch of the Moose, Main and West Branch of Oswegatchie, Raquette, Rock, East, Main and West Branches of the St. Regis, East, Main and West Branches of the Sacandaga, Salmon, Main Branch of Saranac, Schroon, West Canada Creek, South Branch West Canada Creek and West Stony Creek.

WILDLIFE OF SPECIAL CONCERN IN THE ADIRONDACKS

These wildlife species are either endangered, threatened, or "of special concern," meaning that exact status is not determined, but there is reason to believe the species soon could face extinction within the Adirondack region.

The list does not include species already extinct, including the wolf, cougar, lynx and others.

Mammals: Indiana bat, small-footed bat.

Birds: Bald eagle, golden eagle, peregrine falcon, loggerhead shrike, red-shouldered hawk, northern harrier, common tern, osprey, spruce grouse, Cooper's hawk, common loon, common nighthawk, common raven, least bittern, upland sandpiper, black tern, common barn owl, short-eared owl, sedge wren, eastern bluebird, grasshopper sparrow, vesper sparrow.

Reptiles: worm snake, hognose snake, spotted turtle, timber rattlesnake, bog turtle.

Amphibians: Jefferson salamander, blue spotted salamander, spotted salamander.

Fish: Round whitefish, eastern sand darter, mooneye.

THE 46 HIGHEST PEAKS

The 46 highest peaks of the Adirondacks, with elevations of 4,000' or higher, which are the goals of mountain-climbing "46ers," now actually number 47. Listed at left below are the original 46, with their elevations as measured in 1920, plus MacNaughton—not then thought to be 4,000'. The elevations corrected in 1985 revealed that four of the original 46 are lower than 4,000'. The traditional term "46 peaks" remains accepted usage.

Name	Elev. Measured 1920	Corrected Elev. 1985	Name	Elev. Measured 1920	Corrected Elev. 1985
Marcy	5,344	5,344	Marshall	4,411	4,360
Algonquin	5,112	5,114	Allen	4,345	4,340
Haystack	4,918	4,960	Big Slide	4,255	4,240
Skylight	4,920	4,926	Esther	4,270	4,240
Whiteface	4,872	4,867	Upper Wolf Jaw	4,225	4,185
Dix	4,843	4,857	Lower Wolf Jaw	4,175	4,175
Gray Peak	4,902	4,840	Street	4,216	4,166
Iroquois	4,855	4,840	Phelps	4,175	4,161
Basin	4,825	4,827	Donaldson	4,215	4,140
Gothics	4,738	4,736	Seymour	4,120	4,120
Colden	4,713	4,714	Sawteeth	4,138	4,100
Giant	4,622	4,627	Cascade	4,092	4,098
Nippletop	4,620	4,620	South Dix	4,135	4,060
Santanoni	4,621	4,607	Porter	4,070	4,059
Redfield	4,606	4,606	Colvin	4,074	4,057
Wright	4,585	4,580	Emmons	4,139	4,040
Saddleback	4,530	4,515	Dial	4,023	4,020
Panther	4,448	4,442	East Dix	4,020	4,012
Tabletop	4,440	4,427	Blake Peak	4,000	3,960
Rocky Peak Ridge	4,375	4,420	Cliff	4,000	3,960
Macomb	4,425	4,405	Nye	4,160	3,895
Armstrong	4,455	4,400	Couchsachraga	4,000	3,820
Hough	4,404	4,400	MacNaughton	3,976	4,000
Seward	4,404	4,361			

Above: *From Cascade Mountain to-ward Mt. Algonquin.* GEORGE WUERTHNER

Facing page: *In Essex County.* ALBERT GATES

AMERICAN GEOGRAPHIC PUBLISHING

EACH BOOK HAS ABOUT 100 PAGES, 11" X 8¹/₂", 120 TO 170 COLOR PHOTO-GRAPHS

Enjoy, See, Understand America State by State

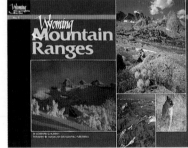

American Geographic Publishing
Geographic Series of the States

Lively, colorful, beautifully illustrated books specially written for these series explain land form, animals and plants, economy, lifestyle and history of each state or feature. Generous color photography brings each state to life and makes each book a treat to turn to frequently. The geographic series format is designed to give you more information than coffee-table photo books, yet so much more color photography than simple guide books.

Each book includes:
• Colorful maps
• Valuable descriptions and charts of features such as volcanoes and glaciers
• Up-to-date understanding of environmental problems where man and nature are in conflict
• References for additional reading, agencies and offices to contact for more information
• Special sections portraying people in their homes, at work, in the countryside

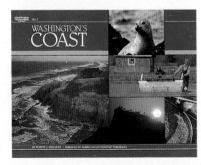

for more information write:
American Geographic Publishing
P.O. Box 5630
Helena, Montana 59604